A SNEAK PEEK
INTO THE
AUDITING
WORLD

INDIA · SINGAPORE · MALAYSIA

Notion Press

No. 8, 3rd Cross Street
CIT Colony, Mylaore
Chennai, Tamil Nadu - 600004

First Published by Notion Press 2020
Copyright © Anupma Aggarwal and Adv (Dr.) Raj Kumar S Adukia 2020
All Rights Reserved.

ISBN 978-1-64899-707-5

A SNEAK PEEK INTO THE AUDITING WORLD

A Day of an Auditor

ANUPMA AGGARWAL
ADV (DR.) RAJ KUMAR S ADUKIA

INDIA · SINGAPORE · MALAYSIA

INDICACADEMY

INDIC PLEDGE

• *I celebrate our civilisational identity, continuity & legacy in thought, word and deed.*

• *I believe our indigenous thought has solutions for the global challenges of health, happiness, peace, and sustainability.*

• *I shall seek to preserve, protect and promote this heritage in doing so,*
  • *discover, nurture and harness my potential,*
  • *connect, cooperate and collaborate with fellow seekers,*
  • *be inclusive and respectful of diverse opinions.*

ABOUT INDIC ACADEMY

Indic Academy is a non-traditional 'university' for traditional knowledge. We seek to bring about a global renaissance based on Indic civilizational and indigenous thought. We are pursuing a multidimensional strategy across time, space and cause by establishing centers of excellence, transforming intellectuals and building an ecosystem.

Indic Academy is pleased to support this book.

Dedication

Dedicated to my father Late CA S.R. Mittal, my ideal, my guru, my mentor.

Contents

About the Authors

Anupma Aggarwal

Anupma Aggarwal is a Chartered Accountant and a member of the Institute of Chartered Accountants. She was a merit holder in CA Intermediate Exams and held 32nd rank in it. She is also SAP Professional in FICO module. She has worked in the capacity of internal auditor and also as Financial and management consultant for US clients

She has been an academician and has the experience of co-authoring books for ACCA and IFRS with an overseas publishing company, Get Through Guides. She also has been in close association in the business world and has taken her home business to great heights

Dr Raj Kumar S Adukia

Dr Rajkumar S Adukia is the founding partner at Adukia and Associates and has more than thirty years of experience in specialized areas such as financial planning, taxation and legal consulting. Dr Adukia holds a degree in law and is a PhD in Corporate Governance in Mutual Fund, an MBA, Diploma in IFRS(UK), Diploma in Labour Laws and Labour Welfare, IPR and Criminology. In addition to being a Chartered Accountant, Company Secretarya and Cost Accountant, he is also an eminent business consultant, advisor, author and speaker.

He is currently a member of the Quality Review Board under the Chartered accountants Act, 1949. He is the only representative from India in IFRS and SMEs Implementation Group (SMEIG) of International Accounting Standards Boards (IABS). He has given innumerable lectures and written more than 300 books on a wide variety of topics ranging from those dealing with IFRS, trade, taxation, finance, real estate to topics like time management and professional opportunities. He has also authored two books on International Financing Reporting Standards.

Preface

This book is a real beginner's book for someone who aspires to learn what auditing is all about. The book is equipped with fundamental auditing concepts and it gives a short glimpse of the auditing world. This book can help any novice in auditing to know what to look forward to in the auditing world and can kick-start his/her journey in the auditing world.

It is a guide for the business owners to get information about the education, training, certification and experience of the stranger who walks into your business asking about private accounting and auditing facts. Fresh auditors and auditing students can get an initiation into the types of tasks they are expected to perform during a typical day on the job.

Auditing involves investigating information prepared by others to decide whether the information is fairly stated. We see all people audit to some extent in their personal lives. A simple form of auditing adopted by all in day to day life is checking your bank account to make sure all transactions are correct. This book is about audit of financial statements and has a similar goal to ensure all the financial statements prepared by managers of companies are fair and true.

Chapter 1

Evolution of Audit

Introduction

We see people constantly checking up on accounts and other activities that make up our daily life. This process is unconsciously done normally. The accounts become object of explicit checking in cases of doubt, conflict and mistrust. We check our restaurant bills, go to the reference library, take a second medical opinion and take references for a prospective employee and so on. Our methods of checking are diverse in different cases.

Is it possible to imagine a society with no checking at all and where all accounts are taken at face value? This is very difficult to conceptualise. When a trading partner does not pay or the restaurant bill makes a mistake or my bank collapses, is it not silly to not check and keep trusting? In short, all persons audit to some extent in their personal lives.

1.1 Evolution of Audit

The term has been derived from the Latin term 'audire', which means to hear.

Audit is as old as accounting. In earlier days, an auditor used to listen to the accounts read over by an accountant in order to check them. It was used in all ancient countries such as

Mesopotamia, Greece, Egypt, Rome, UK and India. The Vedas contain reference to accounts and auditing. Arthasashastra by Kautilya gave rules for accounting and auditing of public finances.

The original aim of auditing was to detect and prevent errors and fraud. It was during the advent of Industrial Revolution, from 1750 to 1840, that auditing began its evolution into a field of detection of fraud and financial accountability.

The different stages of advent of auditing are as below;

<u>Prior to 1840</u>

Auditing was found to be prevalent in the ancient civilization of China, Egypt and Greece. Earlier practices of auditing though not well documented were a proof of the existence of auditing. The first recorded auditors were the spies of King Darius of ancient Persia (522 to 486 B.C.). It was in 1949, Luca Pacioli published the book on double entry bookkeeping system of accounting used by merchants in Venice, Italy. This was the first book on accounting.

1840s to 1920s

It was in 1844 that the British parliament passed the Joint Stock Companies act. The Act required that directors should report to shareholders via an audited financial statement, the Balance sheet. However, the auditor was not required to be an Accountant in 1844. It was in 1900, a new Companies Act was passed that required an independent auditor.

In 1854, the first public accountants organization was the Society of Accountants in Edinburg. The American Association of Public Accountants was formed in 1887, which later became

American Institute of certified Public Accountants (AICPA). The auditing was transaction oriented until 1930 and the procedures were largely based on internal evidence.

1920s to 1960s

Due to excessive misleading financial reporting that led to the stock market crash of 1929, US practice evolved which led to process of collecting evidence as to assets and liabilities or what is called balance sheet audit. The U.S. Securities Acts of 1933 and 1934 created the Securities and Exchange Commission (SEC), which regulated the major stock exchanges in the United states. These legislations greatly influenced auditing around the world.

The companies wishing to trade shares on the New York Stock exchange or the American Stock exchange were required to issue audited income statements as well as Balance Sheets.

1960s to 1990s

In the 1970s, a change in audit approach was observed from 'verifying transactions in the books' to relying on system'. This change was due to the increase in the number of transactions which resulted from the continued growth in size and complexity of companies as it was difficult for auditors to verify all transactions. So, much reliance was placed on companies' internal control system and this reduced the level of detailed substantive testing if internal control was effective.

However, in 1980s, there a shift in auditors' approaches where the assessment of internal control was found costly and so greater use of analytical procedures were used.. An extension of this was the development during the mid-1980s of risk based auditing. Risk-based auditing is an audit approach where an auditor will focus on those areas which are more likely to contain errors.

1990s to Present

Various accounting scandals were seen in the early 2000s like WorldCom, Enron, Tyco etc. Hence, Enron fall Sarbanes-Oxley Act 2002 was passed, which brought accountability provisions for both management and auditors. The Act extended the duties of the auditor to audit the adequacy of internal controls over financial reporting. These scandals led to the fall of the Arthur Anderson, one of the big five audit firm at that time.

The overall audit objectives have although remained the same over time, however critical changes have been made in audit practices as a result of extensive reforms in various countries.

Chapter 2

Fundamentals of Auditing

Introduction

The end products of any formal accounting system are financial statements i.e. income statement and the statement of affairs. These statements are used by various interested parties while making decisions. These statements have to be authentic, truthful and fair so that the interested parties can rely on them. A thorough appraisal of the books of accounts and financial statements are needed taking into consideration the possibility of unintentional mistakes or errors. Auditing comes to the rescue and helps in appraisal of financial statements.

The newer scope of audit goes beyond the fundamental appraisal of financial statements. In today's world, auditing plays a multifaced role in all the functional areas of an organisation.

2.1   Definition

The ICAEW has issued guidelines and Explanatory Foreword to the Auditing Standards. It defines audit in the following terms:

"An audit is the independent examination of, and expression of opinion on, the financial statements of an enterprise by an appointed auditor in pursuance of that appointment and in compliance with any relevant statutory obligation."

It is the process of examining the financial records of an organisation to ensure that they are accurate and in accordance with accounting standards and rules.

2.2   Nature of Audit

The nature of an audit is as follows:

i)   Audit is a systematic examination of the books of account of the business.

ii)   It is undertaken by an independent person or persons who are qualified for job.

iii)   It is a verification of results shown by the profit and loss account and the statement of affairs as shown by the balance sheet.

iv)   It is done with the help of vouchers and documents.

2.3   Objective

The basic objective of an audit is to perform an effective and efficient audit. An audit is effective if the auditor can express his opinion in accordance to the statutory requirement and also comply with the terms of engagement. An audit is efficient if the auditor achieves the best use of assistance provided to him by his client alongwith his expertise and time.

The objectives of an audit can be grouped in three categories:

i)   **Primary Objective**

The main aim is to assess the accuracy and reliability of the financial statements of a particular accounting period and to express an opinion about the truthfulness and fairness of the financial statements.

ii) **Secondary objectives**

The secondary objectives of audit are detection of errors and frauds. Decoding errors may or may not be easy. However, frauds are committed intelligently and auditor can detect frauds if he applies reasonable skill and care. He can also suggest ways to prevent frauds.

iii) **Social objectives**

The social objectives can be listed as below:

- To curb tax evasion
- To protect shareholders' interest
- To ensure fair return to investors
- To comply with the norms and standards
- Comply with policies regarding Corporate Social Responsibility

2.4   Need For Audit

It is necessary to maintain accurate books of accounts while running a business. The more prosperous and busier a business becomes, the need to maintain proper books of accounts is needed. Regular auditing is the way to achieve it.

The reasons for auditing financial statements arise from:

1. **To provide reliability** – The tax officials, financial institutions and the management can all benefit from an

independent financial audit. They can rely on the accuracy of the financial statements and can make decisions accordingly. It is a tool for the management to tighten up their staff and inform their own audits and reports.

2. **To ensure accountability** – As a business grows, it is more important to keep a track of who is accountable for what. There is no substitute for getting financial statements audited to crosscheck performance.

3. **Gives reasonable assurance** – A well carried out audit can give a level of assurance to the investors, tax officials and other external parties such as creditors those are associated with the organisation and have vested interest in its proper functioning.

4. **Provide a complete report** - Auditing financial statements will ensure that there will be an access to comprehensive and up- to-date information when you require.

5. **Can help to boost value and credit rating of business** – Audited financial statements can enhance the value of business. It will improve the credit rating of business, thereby becomes easier to get loans from banks.

Audit can be carried by an external independent auditor, who is then able to report on the accuracy of the financial statements but it can also be maintained internally.

1) **Benefits of External Audit:**

External Audit benefits the users in many ways:

Directors

- Better issues related to corporate governance

- Better reliability on the audited financial statements
- Better adherence to Corporate laws
- Better management of financial issues such as solvency and internal controls.

Owners/ Shareholders

- Better assessment of management performance
- An independent assessment of business

Management

- Better management decisions
- Better management of financial risks
- Better internal financial discipline

Financiers

- Better credit rating
- Better loan worthy

2) **Benefits of Internal Audit**
- Improve operational efficiency
- Reduce the possibility of fraud
- Help in protection of assets
- Increased reliability and integrity
- Ensure adherence to statutory compliances

2.5   Principles Governing An Audit

The basic principles governing an audit are:

i)   **Confidentiality** : The auditor should not disclose any information to the third party and should keep confidentiality of the information.

ii)   **Integrity, Objectivity and Independence**: The auditor has to be fair, honest, impartial in his approach to professional work.

iii)   **Documentation**: The auditor should document matters to show that the audit was carried on as per standards.

iv)   **Audit Evidence**: The auditor should gather enough audit evidence to draw reasonable conclusions thereon.

v)   **Being responsible of work by staff**: The auditor should carefully oversee and review work done by his staff.

vi)   **Professional skill and competence:** The auditor should exercise professional skill and diligence while carrying audit work.

Chapter 3

Audit Cycle

An audit cycle comprises of the following steps:

1. Audit Engagement
2. Knowing the Clients business
3. Audit Plan and audit evidence
4. Substantive and analytical process
5. Audit report

We will study about them in detail below.

3.1   Audit Engagement

According to SA -210, "Agreeing the Terms of Audit Engagement', an auditor should agree with the client to the terms of audit engagement prior to the commencement of the audit. The agreed terms should be then recorded in an engagement letter.

3.1.1 Contents of Audit Engagement Letter

An audit engagement letter should contain the following:

i)   The scope and objective of audit of financial statements

ii)   The responsibilities of the auditor

iii)   The responsibility of the management with regards to selection and application of accounting policies, preparation of financial accounts on a going concern basis, maintenance of accounting records and internal control and written representation by the management

iv)   Arrangement ensuring the involvement of internal auditor and other people and access to all records and documentations

v)   Possibility of fraud remaining undetected

vi)   Identifying applicable financial reporting framework for the preparation of financial statements

3.2   Knowing the Client's Business

The key to an effective and efficient audit is a detailed understanding of the client's business. The Auditing Guideline 'Planning, Controlling and Recording' issued by ICAEW states, " In order to plan his work adequately, the auditor needs to understand the nature of the business of the enterprise, its organisation, its method of operating and the industry in which it is involved, so that he is able to appreciate which events and transactions are likely to have a significant effect on the financial statements."

Understanding client's business helps the auditor to interpret the results of tests and distinguish between significant and insignificant errors. It also helps in developing better professional services. The auditor will know if his advice is relevant to client's needs and enables the auditor to identify those areas in which a client could be expected from a service.

3.2.1 What an auditor needs to know

1. Nature of Business and its brief history
    *   Main activities, products, services
    *   Commercial and financial development such as
    a. History of ownership
    b. History of product
    c. Changes in activities
    d. Other major events such as major acquisitions, major industrial disputes, stock market fluctuations etc

2. Features of the industry
    *   Nature of the industry
    *   Economic factors those affect the industry (consumer disposal income, competing products, seasonal demand)
    *   Position held by the company in the industry (market share, names of major competitors, growth potential)
    *   Dependence on major market and products
    *   Long term trends
    *   Government regulations

3. Products and production
    *   Description of main product lines
    *   Number of products and product range
    *   Relative volume
    *   Plant capacity
    *   Research and development

- Plant capacity
- Management knowledge regarding production planning and control and constraints on mix of products

4. Organisation and location
   - List of companies with its branches and its subsidiaries
   - Description of properties acquired
5. Purchases
   - Types of purchase
   - Names of suppliers
   - Pricing policy
   - Creditors
   - Management knowledge of purchase budget and creditors analysis
6. Sales
   - Pricing policy
   - Name of customers
   - Names of debtors
   - Credit policy
   - Selling methods
   - Marketing strategy
7. Stock
   - Type of stock such as raw material, work in progress and finished goods
   - Quantity held
   - Location of stock
   - Risk factors like shrinkage

- Information like budgeted stock levels, slow moving items and stocktake report

8. Plant and machinery
   - Nature of plant and its value
   - Locations
   - Management data regarding its age, current value, residual value

9. Investments such as major investments and their source

10. Financing such as shares, debentures etc

11. Management team

   - Senior management
   - Employee numbers
   - Types such as full or part time, casual labour
   - Methods of remuneration like salaried, weekly, overtime, holidays
   - Benefits such as pension scheme

12. Professional advisers

   - Lawyers
   - Solicitors
   - Registrars
   - Tax advisers

The above list is comprehensive and is applicable to all types of businesses. It takes time to gather these details and so the auditor discusses with the management what details will be relevant to the client. It has to be seen whether the information is readily available and where required, will be requested to prepare the information so needed.

3.2.2 Sources

The sources from where the auditor gets knowledge of business is:

i)   The client's annual report to shareholders
ii)   Minutes of meeting of shareholders and board of directors
iii)   Previous year audit working papers and relevant files
iv)   Internal financial management report for current and previous year
v)   Discussion with client regarding change in management, current government regulations, current business developments, recent change in technology, change in accounting practices and policies
vi)   Change in accounting policies and procedures
vii)   System of internal control

3.3   Audit Planning

Every auditor should prepare a well organised audit plan before the start of an audit of the client's business. Such a planning is very important for the efficient and effective completion of audit work. It will be required not only for the first engagement but also for the subsequent engagement in the same organisation.

Audit Planning has two objectives:

i)   To ensure efficient conduct of audit work in an efficient manner and cost effective manner

ii)   To ensure maintenance of highest standards and reduce risk of lapses

3.3.1 Activities to be included in audit planning

According to SA 300,'Planning an Audit of Financial Statements', a planning exercise should include the following activities:

i)   To acquire sufficient information regarding the accounting system followed by the client and associated policies

ii)   To assess the internal control system and to decide how much to rely on it

iii)   Determining the nature, scope and timing of various audit procedures.

iv)   To determine the materiality

v)   To obtain a general understanding of the legal and regulatory framework applicable to the entity.

vi)   Use of analytical procedures for risk assessment procedure

vii)   To determine the amount of resources to be deployed in specific audit areas.

viii)   To decide the timing of deploying resources whether at interim stage or at key cut off dates

ix)   To decide how the resources are to be managed

3.3.2 Benefits of Audit Planning

As per SA-300, 'Planning an Audit of Financial Statements', The benefits of audit planning are:

i) It will help the auditor to pay more attention to important areas of audit
ii) It assists the auditor to identify the potential problems and resolve them
iii) It helps in the selection of the audit staff and delegate the work accordingly.
iv) It helps auditor to properly organise and manage the audit engagement
v) It helps in coordination of work done by the auditor of subsidiary if needed.

3.3.3 Considerations in establishing an overall Audit Strategy

As per SA-300, 'Planning an Audit of Financial Statements", an auditor needs to consider quite a few factors while establishing an overall audit strategy. They are as follows:

1) Features of the Engagement

i) The financial reporting framework on which the financial information needs to be audited needs to be prepared.
ii) Industry specific reporting requirement such as reports required by industry regulations.
iii) Relationship between parent and its part and the nature of control and the extent to which the subsidiaries are audited by the auditors.
iv) Statutory audit of standalone financial statements.
v) Nature of business segment to be audited and the need for any specialised knowledge
vi) Availability of work of internal audit and the reliance thereon

2) Audit Timing and nature of Communication

i)   Entity's requirement of reporting such as interim or final

ii)   Discussion with management regarding expected time and types of reports and other communication

iii) Communications with the engagement team

iv)   Other communications with third party

3) Preliminary engagement activities

i)   Determination of materiality as per SA320

ii)   Identification of areas with regards to material misstatements and its impact

iii) Results of previous audit

iv)   Expected use of audit evidence as per previous audit

3.4   Audit Programme

An audit programme is essential before commencement of any audit. An audit programme is an elaborate plan of auditing work to be done, specifying the responsibility of the audit staff and procedure to be followed in verifying each item of the financial statements and giving the estimated time required.

3.4.1 Steps in preparing the audit programme

The general steps involved in preparing and audit programme are:

i)   Determine the extent of examination to be done

ii)   Allot the duties among the audit staff according to their qualification and experience

iii)   Specify the time for completing the allotted responsibilities

iv)   Determine the audit techniques to be followed

3.4.2 Objectives of audit programme

The aim of audit programme is to:

i)   Ensure that important matter is not left out

ii)   Allot the duties to the audit staff according to their qualifications

iii)   To see that audit work is completed on time

iv)   Keeping a record of each work to be done and the progress

3.4.3 Qualities of a good audit programme

A good audit programme has following qualities:

i)   It should include all material items

ii)   It should be flexible to add, change any part of it

iii)   It must be designed to include all functions

iv)   It must be objective oriented

v)   It should be prepared with functions logically arranged

3.4.4 Benefits of a good audit programme

i) Detailed plan of work and timely completion of it

ii) Balanced distribution of work among the audit staff according to their qualification and experience

iii) Audit programme help in assessing progress of work done by the staff

iv) It provides the details of work and any deviations can be quickly identified

v) It can be used as documentary evidence to defend any allegations of professional negligence later

3.4.5 Disadvantages of audit programme

i) The audit work becomes mechanical and staff loses interest. The effectiveness of audit gets reduced

ii) Audit programmes sometimes become unrealistic as regards to the completion of job and hence, it is compromised.

iii)A fixed audit programme is boring to follow and staff loses enthusiasm

3.5   Audit Working Paper

An auditor adopts different methods and procedures and thereafter analyses audit evidence and other essential documents regarding his engagement. Audit working paper includes all such records during the course of work. Such records can be in physical or an electronic form.

As per SA-230, 'Audit Documentation' also called as audit working paper refers to the record of audit procedures performed, relevant audit evidence obtained and conclusions reached.

3.5.1 Purpose of Audit Working Paper

As per SA-230 'Audit Documentation', audit documentation serves many purposes:

i)   Gives evidence that audit was performed as per Standards

ii)   Gives evidence of auditor's basis of conclusion about the achievement of the overall objectives of the auditor

iii)   This assists engagement team to plan and perform the audit and be accountable for its work

iv)   Helping in the conduct of quality control review s per SQC1

v)   Assisting in the conduct of external inspection as per applicable legal requirements

3.5.2 Contents of Audit Working Paper

As per SA-230, an auditor should perform the guidelines mentioned below:

i)   The auditor should prepare audit working papers on a timely basis

ii)   The auditor shall prepare audit working papers to understand:

a)The nature, timing and extent of audit procedures to comply with

b) the results of the audit procedure performed and the evidence obtained

c) important matters arising during the audit

ii) While documenting the nature of the audit procedures, the auditor shall record

a)the identifying features of the specific matter

b)the date of audit work and who performed it

c)who reviewed the audit work and the date and extent of this review

iv) The auditor shall also document discussions of important matters with management and those charged with governance.

v)If the auditor identified information that is inconsistent with the auditor's conclusion, the auditor shall document the same

vi)In case the auditor judges it necessary to depart from the requirement in a SA, the auditor shall document how the alternative audit procedure performed achieved and the reasons of departure

3.5.3 Preservation of Audit Working Paper

Audit working papers being important documents are of continuing importance and can be used for future. These can be used by the auditor to defend any allegations of professional negligence. Hence, the relevant audit working papers must be filed and preserved for a sufficient period of time to meet auditor's need and for future reference also.

3.5.4 Confidentiality of Audit Working Paper

Audit documentation are very important paper and contain important information of the organisation structure and accounting policies of an entity. This data may be of high value for the competitors and once leaked can be misused. These audit working papers need to be kept in safe custody and not made available to the third party except with the permission of the client.

3.5.5 Ownership and custody of Audit Working Papers

While understanding the need for preserving and maintaining audit paper's confidentiality, the question that arise is that who is the owner and custodian of the audit working paper. One view is that the audit working paper is the property of the client as papers are made on the basis of client's book of accounts and other documents provided by him. The other view is that they belong to the auditor as they are papers prepared by the auditor while discharging his duties. The auditor can defend himself against future allegations against him.

This conflict has been resolved by the professional bodies through different regulatory pronouncements. As per SA-230, 'Audit Documentation', audit working papers are the property of auditor and not the client. The auditor can hand over them to the client on request if he wants but he cannot be compelled to do so. The auditor need to maintain a high degree of confidentiality regarding the same and preserve them for considerable period of time to meet the practice and the legal requirements.

3.6 Audit Files

An audit file is used by the auditor to preserve all important documents relevant for the audit of an organisation. It acts as the archive of all important statements, notes etc during the audit of the organisation.

The audit file is very important as it can be used as a reference. It can be used any charge of professional negligence brought against the auditor by the client or the third party.

3.6.1 Classification of Audit File

Audit files are of two types:

- Permanent Audit File
- Temporary Audit File

Permanent Audit file

It contains all the documents which are of continuing importance for the audit of succeeding years. It includes:

i)Name, address and contact information of the client

ii)Documents describing the organisational structure of the client's business. They include memorandum of association and articles of association in case of a company, partnership deed in case of a firm etc.

iii)Certified copies of important legal documents

iv)Copies of various important instructions issued by the management

v)Communication record with previous auditor

vi)Significant ratio and trends analysis

vii)Certified copies of shareholders meetings and board meetings

viii)Certified copies of audited accounts of previous year

ix)Significant audit observations of earlier years

x)Letter to ex-auditor

Temporary Audit File

It contains documents relevant for the audit of the current year only. It includes:

i)Documents related to changes incorporated in the audit programme considering the changes in the internal control system and accounting policies and procedures.

ii)Audit memorandum, audit plan and programme of current year

iii)Audit evidences during course of audit

iv)Various analytical statements prepared during the course of current audit

v)Internal control questionnaire and flow charts

vi) Different accounting schedules such as schedule of creditors, debtors and contingent liabilities

viii)Copies of queries raised during the audit

ix)Letters of representation or confirmation received from the client

x)Auditor's conclusion related to important matters

3.7 Audit Evidence

As per SA -500, 'Audit Evidence', the term 'audit evidence' includes information used by the auditor in arriving at the conclusion on which the audit opinion is based. It includes both information contained in the accounting records underlying the financial statements and other information.

3.7.1 Need of audit evidence

In SA-200, it is seen that reasonable assurance is obtained when the auditor has obtained sufficient and appropriate audit evidence in order to reduce risk.

The auditor should obtain sufficient and appropriate audit evidence and analyse them before arriving at any opinion. This will ensure to keep the audit risk to substantially low level.

3.7.2 Types of audit Evidence

Audit evidence is of two types:

A. Internal evidences

These are evidences collected from within the organisation such as sales invoice, goods received note, debit and credit note

B External evidence

These are evidence collected from outside sources such as purchase invoice, debtors and creditors confirmation.

3.7.3 Reliance and reliability of audit evidence

The audit evidence must be relevant and reliable in order to assess the truthfulness and fairness of the financial statements.

According to SA-500, the relevance of audit evidence deals with the audit procedures and its testing. Also, the reliability of audit evidence depends upon its source whether internal or external and nature whether visual, oral or documentary. However, the following things need to be considered while assessing the reliability of audit evidence:

i) Evidence from external and independent sources are more reliable.

ii) When the internal controls are more effective, internal evidence becomes more reliable.

iii) Evidence in written form is more reliable than oral representation.

iv) Direct evidences obtained by the auditor is more reliable than indirect.

v) Evidence obtained by original documents is more reliable than audit evidence by photocopies.

An auditor should try to obtain evidences from various sources. In case of any discrepancy, the auditor must obtain additional evidence by conducting other audit procedures.

3.7.4 Different methods of obtaining audit evidence

The following are the methods of obtaining audit evidence:

i)   **Inspection:** Inspection involves examining records or documents, whether internal or external, in paper form or otherwise. It can provide effective reliable audit evidence depending upon the internal control over their generation and processing. One of the example is to physically examine the tangible asset for confirming its existence and inspecting the title deeds.

ii)   **Observation:** It is an act of looking at a procedure done by others on a real time basis. An example is to observe the inventory counting by the employees.

iii)   **Mathematical accuracy:** Mathematical accuracy can be checked manually or electronically.

iv)   **Confirmation from outside party:** Any confirmation from third party like customer or supplier can be obtained in paper form or electronically.

v)   **Analytical Procedures:** They involve proper evaluation of financial information by studying possible relationships between financial and non-financial data and investigating fluctuations from previous year.

vi)   **Enquiry:** It involves seeking information, both financial and non-financial, from within or outside the entity.

3.7.5 Audit procedures required for audit evidence

As per SA-315 and SA-330, audit evidence to draw reasonable conclusions is obtained by performing:

i)   Risk assessment procedures
ii)   Further audit procedures which comprise:
        a)Compliance Procedures
        b)Test of details and analytical procedures known as Substantive Procedures

Risk assessment procedures are done to obtain an understanding of the entity and its environment, to identify and assess the risk of material misstatement at the financial statement and assertion level.

It includes the following:

i)   Enquiries of management

ii)   Analytical procedures to identify aspects of the entity the auditor is not aware of

iii)   Observation and inspection

Compliance procedure is the audit procedure designed to evaluate the operating effectiveness of controls in preventing and rectifying material misstatements at the assertion level. It includes the following:

i)   To check if internal control exists

ii)   The control system is working effectively

iii)   If control has operated throughout audit period

Lastly, substantive procedure is the audit procedure designed to detect material misstatements by either test of detail like vouching and verification or by analytical procedures like analysis of significant ratios and trends

3.8   Substantive And Analytical Procedures

3.8.1 Substantive Procedures

Substantive procedures are those activities carried out by the auditor to detect material misstatement or fraud at the assertion level. These procedures are the steps taken by the auditor to obtain evidence regarding:

i)   The transactions during the year

ii)   The balances of the assets and liabilities as at the end of the year

The different assertions of transactions are:

- Occurrence
- Completeness
- Authorization
- Accuracy
- Cut-off
- Classification

The different assertions of balances are:

- Existence
- Validity
- Rights and obligations
- Completeness

Few examples of main substantive procedures

The following are the examples of main substantive procedures:

1)**Vouching** It is the audit procedure used in order to obtain evidence regarding the transactions during the accounting year. The auditors obtain evidence to prove that the transactions actually occurred and all transactions are accounted, disclosed properly and recorded for the right amount.

2) **Checking posting:** The auditor has to check whether the right amount is posted in the right amount and on the right side of the account.

3) **Ledger scrutiny:** It is the procedure and review of the accounts of parties, liabilities, income and expenses in different types of ledger.

4)**Verification:** It is the procedure to check various balances of all accounts as at the end of the year. It involves physical inspection, confirmation

5) Grouping and disclosures: It involves:

i) Checking the ledger balances with the trial balance

ii) Checking if the items are properly disclosed in the final statements

3.8.2 Methods of Substantive Testing

Substantive Tests fall into four categories:

- Inspection of documents
- Inspection of assets
- Direct confirmation
- Reperformance of computation

a) Inspection of documents

The main method of verifying the nature and validity of a transaction or an account item is by inspecting related documents and records. It is important to not only check the amount involved agrees and all details like address, names, dates, price and description of goods and services are correct.

Considerations should also be given to whether the document inspected provides supporting evidence and whether all the documents that would normally be expected are available. Photocopies are not considered adequate verification.

b) Inspection of assets

Physical inspection is a means of verifying the existence and possession of an asset; it will be needed to obtain other evidence before concluding as to the ownership of the asset. For example, physical inspection of a factory, plant and machinery will verify that they exist but the factory may be mortgaged.

c)Direct Confirmation

Written confirmation from third parties can provide strong evidence of the validity of balance and transactions. The value placed on third party evidence must take into account the status of the person giving the confirmation and the evidence available to them.

d)Reperformance of computation and reconciliation

It is important to understand the principles of the calculation and to check the underlying assumptions to verify arithmetical accuracy. We need to reperform a reconciliation in order to verify an item.

3.8.3 Analytical Procedures

Analytical procedures are the process to carefully study the relationship between various financial and non-financial data, analysing their behaviour to identify any unusual deviation from the expected value of the item or any inconsistency with relevant information and the reason thereof. As per SA-520 on "Analytical procedures', analytical procedure means evaluation of financial information through analysis of plausible relationship among both financial and non- financial data.

3.8.4 Nature of Analytical Procedures

As per SA520, the nature of analytical procedures include the following:

i)It includes comparison of entity's financial information with

a) Comparable information of prior periods

b)Any anticipated results such as budget or forecast or estimate of depreciation

c)Similar data of any other comparable entity belonging to the same industry or the industry averages

ii) It may also include consideration of relationships

a)Among different items of financial data that is expected to follow a particular pattern like operating profit margin

b)Between financial and non-financial data like the number of employees and the total compensation cost.

iii) Analytical procedures consider application of diverse analytical tools those may range from simple comparison to complex analysing

iv)They may be applied either on standalone or consolidated financial statements.

3.8.5 Application of Analytical procedures

As per SA520, analytical procedures can be applied at different stages of the audit work,

i)Audit Planning

The auditor may apply analytical procedures to have an understanding of the client's business. He may use this data in determining the nature, timing and extent of other procedures such as routine checking or vouching,

ii)Substantive Test

The auditor may apply substantive analytical procedure either alone or in combination with the test of detail.

iii)Overall conclusion

The auditor may also apply the analytical procedures to assess how far the conclusions drawn on financial statements are consistent and whether there is need to revise them.

iv)Unusual items

If the analytical procedures performed identify any inconsistency in relationships, the auditor should investigate items by inquiring the management or by collecting further evidences and by performing other audit procedures.

3.8.6 Techniques of Analytical Procedures

It includes application of the following tools:

a) Trend Analysis

It analyses any fluctuations in the amount of any account by comparing current year's figure with that of the preceding years.

b) Testing of Reasonableness

This is done by analysing the relationship of certain items or account balances with other balances. Few examples are:

i) Work in progress based on material based

ii) Raw material consumption to production

iii) Percentage of wastage and scrap

iv) Sales commission against sales volume

v) Interest expenses against interest bearing obligations

c) Ratio Analysis

It includes different ratios between various items of financial statements in order to study their relationships such as Gross profit ratio, inventory turnover ratio, net profit ratio

d) Sources of information

It requires analysing the following sources of information:

- Budgets
- Management Accounts
- VAT returns
- Board minutes

3.8.7 Extent of reliance of analytical procedures

As per SA520, reliability of analytical procedures depend upon these factors:

a)The reliability of analytical procedures are likely to be more reliable when it is based on independent outside sources

b)It is more reliable when the data of the client is compared with the data of industry.

c)Analytical procedures should be based on standards than rational.

d)Regular items are mostly reliable and likely to have definite relationships with other regular items

e)Material items should be carefully handled.

3.9   Audit Report

An audit report is a document written in a standard format through which the auditor expresses his opinion regarding the reliability and correctness of an entity's financial statements.

It would be discussed in later chapter.

Chapter 4

Audit Sampling and Audit Procedures

4.1 Audit Sampling

In case of large firms, it is neither feasible nor possible to verify each and every transaction to come to a conclusion relating to true and fair view of financial performance and its affairs. The auditor should apply partial checking to form its opinion. However, the success of partial checking depends on appropriate sample selection. Hence, it is important that the auditor should have sufficient knowledge regarding sampling technique.

According to SA-530 on 'Audit Sampling' issued by ICAI, auditing is the process of selecting a limited number of transactions out of the total transactions of a given category using a reasonable basis and thereby applying the audit procedures on the selected transactions to form an opinion thereof.

4.1.1 Purpose of Audit Sampling

The need for audit sampling is:

i)   Audit sampling helps to reduce the working load of the auditor without compromising the audit quality

ii)   Audit work based on sampling saves cost and time

iii) The success of audit based sampling technique largely depends upon the outcome of the internal control.

iv) Audit based sampling technique produces results close to reality.

v) The auditor saves time in limited checking and thus gets more time to engage in innovative audit procedures.

4.1.2 Factors to be considered for Audit Sampling

The following factors have to be considered for designing an audit sample:

i)The auditor needs to consider the purpose to be achieved and the audit procedures best suited for this purpose.

ii)The auditor must consider the nature of the population i.e. the degree of homogeneity of its items.

iii)The auditor should also evaluate the adequacy of the internal control system. In the event of an inadequate internal control system, the sample size needs to be larger in order to be representative of the whole.

iv)The auditor needs to consider only material items those would change the final result.

v)Audit sample must be designed to keep the sampling risk within the acceptable limit.

vi)The auditor must take due care to avoid any personal bias while collecting and analysing sample data.

4.1.3 Techniques of sampling

There are broadly two techniques of sampling

- Statistical Sampling

- Non-statistical Sampling

The discretion whether to use statistical or non-statistical sampling depends upon the auditor himself. The auditor must keep in mind that the sample must be representative, otherwise the basic objective of sampling will not be attained.

1.Statistical Sampling

It is a scientific approach and is not dependable on the auditor's discretion. It applies mathematical laws of probability in determining the appropriate sample size. This approach is extremely useful when there are large number of similar transactions.

It is more accurate technique but it requires specialised knowledge on the part of audit staff.

2. Non Statistical Sampling

In this technique, the sample size and its composition are determined based on auditor's own experience and knowledge. It is not a scientific technique and depends upon the discretion of auditor's experience and judgement. This method is simple and easy to execute but does not require the knowledge of statistics.

Statistical sampling has an edge over non-statistical sampling due to the scientific approach.

4.1.4 Sample selection Methods

The sample should be representative of the population from which it is being selected. There are various steps to fulfil this basic objective:

i)Random Sampling

In this method of sampling, each item of the population has a known chance of selection. Random sampling can be of two types:

a)Simple Random Sampling

Each unit of the population has an equal chance of being selected in the sample under this method. Here selection is normally done either choosing a random number manually from the random number table or allowing the computer programme to select a random number and then identifying the population unit that corresponds to the random number by using any predefined rule. This method normally requires the population to be reasonably homogeneous.

b) Stratified Sampling

This method requires a given heterogeneous population to be first divided into a number of sub-populations with homogeneous items. Then equal or unequal proportion of items from each group are selected to form a representative sample of reasonable size. For example,

Trade payable balances may be divided into four groups

- Balances upto 10000
- Balances in between 10000 and 50000
- Balances between 50000 and 100000
- Balances above 100000

The auditor may plan to vouch for all transactions in first group, 25% in second, 50% in third and 10% in fourth. He may decide to pick up equal percentage in each group.

ii)Systematic Sampling

This method requires selecting constant interval between selections with the first selection being random. The interval can be based on a number or monetary value like 20th of an item or Rs20000 of cumulative purchases.

Systematic sampling can be of two types:

a)Block Sampling

This method requires selection of a defined block of consecutive items. The auditor may select first 50 entries of the sales book for the month of June or any two blocks of 25 purchase items from June. Hence, once the first item is selected, the next 25 items of the block will normally follow it for selection. This method is simple and economical.

b)Cluster Sampling

The population is first divided into number of groups known as clusters in this method such as purchase and sales invoice are kept in months. The auditor then selects a number of clusters randomly using random number tables.

iii)Monetary Unit Sampling

This method uses the monetary value of the transaction as the basis of sample size determination. It is known as value-based sampling.

iv)Multi-stage Sampling

This method is suitable when data are stored in more than one level. A firm may have stored at a number of branches. Here, the first step would be to randomly select a few branches and then to randomly select a few items from the branch.

v)Haphazard Sampling

The auditor selects items without following any structured rule. Haphazard sampling is appropriate only for non-statistical sampling.

4.1.5 Risk associated with audit sampling

The risk associated with sampling can be divided into two categories:

i) Sampling risk

Sample is only selected part of the population, so it can never reflect all the features of the population. Therefore, results obtained from that based on entire population irrespective of the sample size or the method applied for sample selection. Audit sampling is subject to this error and the corresponding risk is known as sampling risk.

As per SA-530, sampling risk is divided into two categories:

a) Sampling risk associated with compliance procedure

Compliance procedure of the organisation.is the process of evaluation of the internal control system. The auditor faces two kinds of risks while applying compliance procedure. They are:

i)The auditor may conclude that the controls are more effective while they are not. They may be called the risk of over reliance. This can lead to inappropriate report.

ii)The auditor may also find that the controls are less effective while they are not. This is the risk of under reliance.

b) Sampling risk associated with Substantive Procedures

Substantive procedures is the process of evaluation of the validity and appropriateness of the data generated through the system of recording. Of transactions. The auditor faces two kinds of risks:

i)The auditor may conclude there are no misstatements while they do exist. This is known as risk of wrong acceptance.

ii)Otherwise, the auditor may conclude that there are material misstatements while they do not exist. This is called risk of wrong rejection.

Both the above risks should be avoided to ensure quality of audit work.

ii) Non Sampling Risk

Non-sampling error may arise due to improper processing of data if done by inexperienced audit staff. If audit is done by experienced staff, then the non sampling risk may be reduced to zero.

Non-sampling risk is avoidable while sampling risk is unavoidable. The auditor can reduce it to the possible extent by adhering to the proper method of sampling.

4.1.6 Stages in Audit Sampling

Audit sampling requires the following steps:

i)The auditor should carefully consider the objectives of sampling and the nature of population units and thus finalise the sampling method. For example Simple random sampling may be used if population are homogeneous.

ii)Sample size should be determined by the application of a statistics based formula to minimise sampling risk.

iii)Sample size needs to be selected that each sample becomes a representative of the population

iv)The auditor then performs audit procedure on each item selected. If the auditor is not able to apply audit procedure on a selected item, it should be performed on a replacement item.

v)The auditor shall identify the nature and cause of misstatement to evaluate its possible impact on the purpose of auditing.

vi)In case of substantive procedure, the auditor must project misstatements found in the sample to the population. However, no explicit projection is required for test of control.

vii)The results of audit sampling should be evaluated. In case of compliance procedures, a high degree of sample deviation will lead to increase in the assessed risk of material misstatements. In case of substantive procedures, an unexpected high misstatement amount may mean that a class of transaction or account balance is materially misstated.

4.2 Audit Procedures

An auditor performs various procedures while conducting an audit of an organisation. Few procedures are applied all the time while few others are used only when situation demands. These are known as Audit Procedures. It entirely depends upon auditor's discretion as to which procedure needs to be used.

Few of the widely used audit procedures are:

i)Routine checking

ii)Test Checking

iii)Detailed Auditing

iv)Cut-of Procedure

v)Rotational Tests

vi)Surprise Checking

vii)Walk through Tests

4.2.1 Routine Checking

Routine checking is the procedure to check whether the transactions are properly entered in the books of accounts. It is done to ensure that mathematical accuracy is maintained while recording transactions in the books of accounts. It helps in detection of frauds and errors.

The purpose of routine checking is:

i)It ensures arithmetical accuracy of books of accounts by checking the accuracy of casting, posting, balancing and carry forward.

ii) It helps to detect unintentional errors and frauds.

iii)It helps in increasing the reliability of Final Accounts.

iv)After an efficient routine checking, subsequent detail audit to identify errors and frauds become easier.

4.2.1.1 Scope of Routine checking

Routine checking comprises of following functions:

i)Checking the correctness of casting and balancing of the books of accounts.

ii)Examining the correctness of posting from the books of primary entry to the books of accounts.

iii)Checking the correctness of casting, balancing and carry forwards of ledger accounts.

iv)Checking the correctness of trial balance

v)Examining the correctness of Final Accounts

4.2.1.2 Benefits of routine checking

- It is simple form of audit work
- It doesn't require special knowledge of accounting theories or legal provisions.
- It helps in ensuring arithmetical accuracy.
- It helps in detection of errors and frauds and thus ensures correctness of Final Accounts

4.2.1.3 Limitations of routine checking

- It can create monotony in checking
- The audit staff not being specialised may be negligent towards work
- This form of checking may not detect all types of errors
- It may fail to detect any frauds and manipulations in the books of accounts

A well-executed routine checking significantly reduces the subsequent workload of the auditor. It is the duty of the auditor to carefully decide the scope and depth of the intended routine checking.

4.2.2 Test checking

Test checking is the selection and examination of a representative sample from a large number of similar items. It is a procedure where a number of representative transactions are selected out of a group of large transactions and in-depth examination is done. The concept of test checking is based on the principle of 'Sampling Theory' in Statistics.

The objectives of test checking are:

- To save cost of audit work
- To complete audit work in limited time
- To draw a valid conclusion on the fairness of accounts

4.2.2.1 Precautions to be taken in test checking

Organisations differ in their set up. As a result, it is difficult to determine any common parameters while performing test checking. The precautions to be applied are:

- The auditor should review the internal control system that will help to decide the scope of test checking
- Transactions selected should cover the different periods of the year
- Transactions selected should cover almost all the employees to some extent
- Transactions should be homogeneous in nature
- Sample size should be adequate
- Selection bases should be constantly changed
- Transactions during the first and last year should be properly checked
- Control accounts should not be test checked

- Selection of transactions should be preferably done by the auditor himself

4.2.2.2 Transactions where test checking is not appropriate

The following transactions are recommended to be outside the scope of test checking:

- Industries subjected to seasonal fluctuations
- Non-recurring transactions
- Transactions with legal implications
- Transactions based on estimates
- Opening entry, closing entry and reconciliations
- Presentations and disclosures under financial statements

4.2.2.3 Benefits and limitations of test checking

The benefits of test checking are:

- The audit work is completed in lesser period of time
- It is done at reduced cost
- It significantly reduces work pressure
- The auditor can take more assignments

The limitations of test checking are:

- Since all transactions are not tested, there is a chance of risk
- It is not suitable for small organisations as internal control system is normally not there
- This procedure may not exhibit a true and fair view of the accounts maintained
- It is sure to fail in case the samples are not true representation of population.

It is true that test checking reduces the workload than routine checking, especially in large organisations. However, there are some risks involved. If test checking is applied without sufficient care, the auditor may be held responsible for professional negligence.

4.2.3 Detailed Auditing

Detailed Auditing refers to the procedure where a few selected transactions are examined from the start till the end. The auditor selects a few representative transactions of material importance and then carries a detailed stage by stage examination.

Detailed auditing is an intermediate approach. It eliminates the limitations of both routine checking and test checking. Routine checking requires detail examination of every transaction which is time consuming and costly. On the other hand, test checking requires examination of a few independently selected transactions which have significant risks.

4.2.3.1 Process of Detailed Auditing

Detailed auditing is the three-step process:

- Firstly, the auditor reviews the effectiveness of the internal control system
- Secondly, a few transactions of material importance are selected
- Finally examination of each and every stage of the execution and recording of the selected transactions is conducted

4.2.3.2 Benefits and limitations of Detailed Auditing

The benefits of detailed auditing are:

- It helps to achieve precision in course of audit work
- Cost of audit can be reduced significantly
- It reduces time required to complete the audit work
- Since transactions of material importance are examined, there is lesser chance of the overall audit report going wrong
- It is very effective in propriety audit

The limitations of detailed auditing are:

- It is not good for small concerns which do not have effective internal control system
- The success of this method mainly depends upon the appropriate sample selection
- It involves risk of non-detection of some frauds and errors.
- There is a chance fraud may be committed in less material transactions

Success of detailed auditing largely depends on an effective internal control system. Any large concern with adequate internal control system is suitable for detailed auditing. The auditor thus needs to first evaluate the existing internal control system of the organisation.

4.2.4 Cut-off Procedure

In case of going concern, transactions occur on a continuous basis. Thus, it is important to apply periodic concept to assess its performance. However, there may be a number of items especially at the end of the accounting year those have impact carried to the next accounting period.

Work in progress, goods in transit, prepaid and outstanding expenses are a few. Improper treatment of these items and inclusion of items relating to one year in the next year may distort the financial results. Hence the auditor should apply definite procedure to separate transactions at the end of one accounting period from those at the start of the next accounting period. Such a procedure is known as Cut -off procedure. Here, the auditor first decides a cut-off date and then examines all the transactions that occurred within a definite time period prior and post cut-off period to discriminate transactions of current period from that of the next period.

The purpose of Cut-off procedure are:

- To separate the transactions of the current year from that of the next year
- To apply the concept of matching revenue with relevant costs
- To ensure that adjustment entries are properly entered
- To enclosure of true and fair view of Final Accounts
- To detect and prevent any error and fraud

4.2.4.1 Factors to be considered in Cut-off Procedure

The factors to be followed in Cut-off Procedure are:

i)Purchase Transactions

The auditor needs to see that purchase includes only those goods whose ownership has already been transferred and the same has been recorded in the stores while calculating the closing stock.

ii)Sales Transactions

The auditor needs to see that sales includes only those goods whose ownership has already been transferred and the same has been deducted from the stores while calculating the closing stock.

iii)Goods in transit

The auditor should see that any goods purchased during the year end for which purchase invoice has been received but the goods have not reached the stores are included in Goods in transit.

iv)Goods on approval

The auditor must see that goods sent to the potential customers on approval basis on which no confirmation is received are included in stock. He needs to ensure that the sales value of such goods is not included in sales or debtors.

v)Prepaid and outstanding expenses

The auditor needs to ensure that the incomes and expenses of a particular year are included in that year only. He has to carefully verify the adjustment of any item of prepaid or outstanding expenses or incomes in the final accounts.

4.2.5 Rotational Tests

Rotational tests are very useful while conducting audit of large organisations with operations located in different geographical locations. They are performed in two way

i)   The auditor visits different factories, branches etc at different locations on rotation so that all locations are covered though not within a single year but over a period of time.

ii)   The auditor conducts general audit of all areas of client's business every year but selects one or two specific areas for detailed checking.

It must be clear that rotational tests are only applicable if the same auditor is engaged for audit over the years.

4.2.6 Surprise Checking

Normally, the auditor generally informs the client of his routine checking and timing of the next visit as well in advance. However, there may be ample scope for any wrong doings whatsoever. Thus it is recommended that an auditor must conduct surprise tests of some material items without any prior intimation to the client. These surprise checks helps to increase the efficiency of the work. Hence surprise checking means that an audit procedure is conducted on a non-routine and surprise basis.

The areas of application of surprise checks are:

- Verification of cash balance
- Verification of stock and stores
- Verification of investments
- Verification of any part of internal control system
- Verification of appropriate maintenance of various statutory books of accounts

4.2.6.1 Recommendations of ICAI regarding surprise checking

Following are the recommendations of ICAI :

i)The auditor needs to decide the scope of surprise checking

ii)Surprise checking must be conducted more than once. Generally, it is considered at least once a year.

iii)The management must immediately inform the errors or frauds detected through surprise checking.

iii)Any inadequacy of internal control system must also be informed to the management.

iv)The results of surprise checking should not be mentioned in the final audit report unless there is any material misstatement found in surprise checking.

4.2.7 Walk through Tests

Walk through test may be defined as tracing one or more transactions through the accounting system and observing how it is actually passed through the internal control system. If the auditor is satisfied about the appropriateness of all relevant stages of the transaction, he may conclude that the internal control is functioning well and plan his audit work accordingly. Then the auditor may decide to put reliance on the system to some extent. In case the walk through test reveals serious weakness in the internal control system, the auditor may opt for verifying a larger sample under test checking or may go for routine checking of all transactions as the case may be.

Conclusion

It is important to tell that the different audit procedures are not a substitute to each other but are complementary. Simultaneous application of a number of procedures to verify different areas of client's accounts is highly recommendable.

Chapter 5

Internal Control including Internal Check and Internal Audit

5.1 Internal Control

Meaning

Internal control system provides a measure for the management to obtain information, protection and control which are needed for the crucial running of a business organisation. It is the total system of control established by the management of an organisation so as to achieve organisational objective effectively and efficiently.

Internal check and internal audit are a part of internal control.

The objectives of internal control are:

i)It is to ensure that all transactions are approved by the responsible personnel in accordance with specific authority

ii)It is to ensure that all transactions are accurately recorded and no valid transaction has been omitted.

iii)It is to ensure that all books of accounts are recorded in all respects iv)It is to ensure that all recorded transactions represent the economic events that actually occurred and have been executed in accordance with general authorisation by the management.

v)It is to ensure that access to physical assets and information systems are controlled

vi)It is to ensure that errors detected at any stage of processing receive prompt corrective action

vii)There has to be segregation of duties. Duties are assigned in a manner that no one individual can control both the recording function and procedures related to processing.

5.1.1 Features of Internal Control

The features of Internal Control are:

i)The best designed internal control can be challenged if the management overrides the controls that are in place. The indicators of an effective control environment include having a whistle-blower hotline or discipline policies that take into consideration the violations seriously.

ii)Risk assessment is assessing the company's business processes that internal control is important. A company's business cycle is examined in great detail in completing a formal risk assessment.

iii)Effective information and communication will include business systems that gather information related to internal control that uses the information to support employees in doing their job.

iv)Monitoring is the ongoing feedback mechanism that ensures that internal control systems that are effectively designed remain that way.

v)Control activities are the specific activities performed by the company personnel to ensure that internal control is effective.

5.1.2 Limitations of internal control

Some limitations are inherent in all internal control system:

i)Control system may become ineffective due to employee collusion.

ii)The total cost of internal control system is often costly.

iii)Internal control system is concerned with common business activities only.

iv)High managerial personnel may override prescribed policies and procedures for personal gain

v)Even well designed internal control system may be a failure due to misunderstood instructions. Errors may also result from new technology and computerised information systems.

5.1.3 Methods of Internal Control by the Auditor

The following are the methods of evaluating internal control system of an organisation:

i)Understanding the internal control system

It is important to understand the internal control system and to see whether it is effective and efficient. This can be collected from various sources like detailed records maintained by the auditor, check lists and internal control questionnaire.

ii)Assessment of Control risk

The internal control system of the organisation may be efficient and effective but still there may be some probability of some material misstatement that cannot be eliminated. Hence evaluation of control risk is necessary to assess the risk associated with the internal control system.

There are some procedures to assess such risks:

a)Examination of documents

b)Enquiries and observations

c)Verification of official documents and charts

If it is found from the control risk assessment that there is high risk of material misstatements in the financial statements, then the auditor should not rely on the internal control system. In case, it is found that if there is no material misstatements, then the auditor can rely on the internal control system.

5.1.4 Section 134(5) of the Companies Act 2013 regarding internal financial controls

Section 134(5) of the Companies Act 2013 require that in case of listed companies, Directors' Responsibility Statement should state that directors had laid down internal financial controls and such controls are adequate and were operating effectively.

5.1.5 Internal control in a computerised environment

Internal control in a computerised environment must differ from internal control in a manual record keeping. The reason is that the application of computers may be easy but it increases the risk substantially.

The two categories of internal control in a computerised environment are:

i)Application controls

Application controls ensure that transactions occurred are authorised and are accurately recorded and processed. Application controls apply to data processing tasks such as sales, purchases and are further classified as:

a)Input Controls

The most common example of programmed controls over the accuracy of input are edit checks by performing:

- Existence check such as the customer's account exists
- Reasonableness check such as net profit to gross profit
- Range check such as advances to labourer are not more than Rs10000

In case of discrepancy, the software will display a screen message for the same.

b)Processing Control

The programmed control over processing is a run to run control. For instance, the opening balance of payables plus the purchase invoice less the cheques paid should be equal to the closing balance of the payables ledger.

c)Master files and standing data control

It requires one for one checking to master files such as product's price changes are checked to an authorised list.

5.1.6 General Controls

These are procedures to establish overall controls. General controls include the following:

a)Management Controls

This control focuses on the policies and procedures relating to the control function of the management.

b)Computer operation control

This ensures that systems are used for authorised purposes and by authorised personnel.

c)System Software and data entry control

This control exercises control over authorisation, testing and approval of software systems. This ensures that entry of transactions in the computer system is duly authorised and is entered by only authorised personnel. Also, there is proper backup of data and data if lost can be recovered.

5.2 Concepts of Internal check

Internal check is a part of internal control and is a means of instituting checks on the day to day transactions which operate continuously as part of the routine system, by means of which work of each individual is checked independently by other. It may be defined as the allocation of duties among the staff so that it eliminates the duplicity of work and also ensures that the work of previous employee is automatically checked by the next one and thus frauds are prevented.

The objectives of internal check are:

- The main aim is to reduce the frauds and errors committed by the staff members.
- It will help to increase the reliability of financial data of an organisation by timely recording of all transactions
- Division of work done ensures smooth flow of work
- It ensures moral pressure over the staff so that they work carefully and continuously
- It helps in finalisation of accounts promptly and helps to improve overall functional efficiency of the concern

5.2.1 Features of internal check

The essential features of an internal check system are:

- It is necessary to divide the work in such a way that the work of one staff can be checked by another. For example, if one staff takes the responsibility of sales, the other should make the payment.
- In today's world, various devices can be used to perform functions automatically like time keeping machines.
- A concern should use self-balancing system of maintaining ledge where errors are detected and rectified easily.
- A concern may transfer the staff from one job to another so that the work of previous staff can be checked by the latter.
- The organisation may arrange for specialised training program to make the staff well equipped.
- Every member should be encouraged to go on special leave at least once a year so that his portion of work is checked by another.

5.2.2 Benefits of Internal Check system

The benefit of Internal Check System are:

- In case the internal check system is effective, an auditor can apply test checks rather than checking the books of accounts and thus save time and cost
- The auditor is able to focus more on critical issues when internal check is sound.
- Internal check is based on the principle of division of labour and thus ensure smooth flow of work.
- There is a moral pressure on employees to remain honest
- It reduces the chances of errors and frauds and facilitates prompt finalisation of work.

5.2.3 Disadvantages of Internal Check System

The demerits of internal control system are:

- As the work of one is checked by another, this may result in conflict among staff members
- Planned frauds with staff involvement may not get detected by internal check
- Employees may become careless thinking their work will be checked by another
- It may not be feasible for small concerns as it involves more manpower.
- Every staff member may pass their responsibility on another.
- There may be collusion among employees or outsiders
- Less internal controls towards unusual transactions
- There may be manipulations by management

5.2.4 Preparation of checklists by the auditor for internal check

The following general checklist may be considered by the auditor:

- No single person should be given control of the entire work
- Compulsory leave should be given to the employee every year
- The duties of the employees should be changed from time to time without previous notice so that the same employee does not perform the same work
- Each and every receipt and dispatch is properly recorded
- Persons having physical custody of assets should not have access to the books of accounts
- Mechanical devices such as automatic cash register should be used for the prevention of cash loss.
- A strict supervision should be exercised to ensure that internal control procedures are fully operative
- Procedures should be laid for periodical verification and testing of different sections of accounting records.

5.2.5 Liability of the statutory auditor for relying on internal check system

Reliance of an effective internal check system and planning the audit process enables the auditor to devote more time on critical areas of accounting. However, such reliance increases the risk of the auditor. The reason is even a sound internal check system cannot guarantee the non-existence of any errors of a detailed checking, there is a chance that errors and frauds remain undetected or fraud in the accounts. In case the auditor uses test checking instead of detailed checking, the auditor cannot escape his responsibility on the plea that he relied on the internal check system.

Thus, the auditor should always keep in mind that resorting to test checking by relying on internal check system doesn't reduce the liability of the statutory auditor. He will be held for negligence if any error or fraud is detected later.

5.2.6 Internal Check System for some transactions

Sales

The internal check regarding cash sales include following steps:

i)Sales counter for different products should be different

ii)Each sales counter should have separate salesman

iii)The salesman can prepare cash memos only and cash memos should be cross-checked by other official

iv)Cash memo should contain pre-printed serial number

v)Cashier after receiving cash payment from the customer should keep one copy of the cash memo and return the other to the customer

vi)There is a separate delivery department from which goods are delivered to customers on producing their copy of cash memo

vii)The gatekeeper takes the perforated portion of customer's copy and the same is given to the authority

vii)A summary of cash sales will be prepared by all the staffs and the same will be submitted to the manager viii)Cash receipt needs to be deposited by head cashier the following day

Stock

i)Different stock levels need to be maintained

ii)The storekeeper needs to place purchase requisition as stock reaches re-order level

iii)It is advisable to maintain optimum level of stock

iv)Goods need to be received by the receiving department and four copies of goods received notes need to be prepared

v)Finished goods received are to be recorded in finished goods ledger.

v)Receiving department should send it to the store after receiving it

vii)Goods to be insured while in store and goods issue to production should be accounted for

viii)Goods returned should be accounted for

ix)Bin card shows the details of goods received and issued should be maintained for each department

x)Accounts department should maintain the store ledger

xi)Obsolete and slow-moving items should be checked and accounting treatment of same should be done

5.2.7 Comparison between Internal Check and Internal Control

Points of comparison	Internal Check	Internal Control
Nature	It is part of internal control	It is the whole system of control
Implementation	Implementation of internal check is the work of regular staff	Internal control is the responsibility of the management staff
Scope of work	It focuses on the work assigned only	It exercises control over all the areas
Importance	It is concerned with record keeping and accounting reports	It is concerned with profitability and productivity of the organisation
Flexibility	It is less flexible	It is more flexible
Internal elements	It has no internal element	It includes internal check and internal audit

5.3 Internal Audit

Internal audit is a continuous checking of the different operational activities of the organisation with an aim to report about the effectiveness of the operations of the organisation. It is also an important part of internal control system.

5.3.1 Purpose of internal audit

As per SA-610, the aim of the internal audit is as follows:

- Review of accounting system
- Review of internal control
- Examination of effectiveness of internal control
- Examination of financial and operating system
- Verification of assets and liabilities
- Conduct special investigation as per management's instructions
- Determine the level of compliance with policies and procedures and government laws and regulations
- Coordinate with external auditors

5.3.2 Functions of Internal Audit

As per the Standard on Audit (SA)-610, 'Using the Work of Internal Auditors', the aim of internal audit functions vary depending on the size and structure of the entity. The functions can be listed as below:

- The internal auditor may be asked to review the economy and effectiveness of operating systems including non-financial activities of the entity.
- The internal auditor may review controls, monitor operations and recommend improvements
- The internal auditor may review compliance with laws, regulations and other management policies
- It is his duty to assist the concern by identifying and evaluating significant exposures to risk.
- It is his duty to see that the organisation follows the ethics and values as laid down by the government.

5.3.3 Benefits of internal audit

The benefits of internal audit are:

- It helps in detection of frauds and errors
- It assists management to execute various plans
- It increases the effectiveness of internal control system
- It ensures whether proper measures have been taken to safeguard the assets
- It is a great assistance to external auditor and helps in reduction of their work

5.3.4 Limitations of internal audit

The limitations of internal audit are:

- It is a costly affair
- It may be difficult for small organisations to carry internal audit due to cost factor
- Internal auditors are employees of the organisation, so it is possible that there may be distortion in reporting
- It is possible that internal audit is carried by inexperienced staff.

5.3.5 Comparison between Internal Control and Internal Audit

Point of comparison	Internal Control	Internal Audit
Nature	It is the whole system of control and its scope is very wide	It is an important part of Internal Control

Time of function	It runs automatically with the execution of transaction	It is not automatic and executed after transaction takes place
Responsibility	It is the responsibility of the management staff	It is executed by the internal auditor
Presence	It is present in all departments	A separate department is made for it
Purpose	To ensure progress of the organisation	To detect errors and frauds

5.3.6 Legal requirement of Internal Audit

According to the section 138 of the Companies Act 2013 read with Rule 13 of Companies (Accounts) Rules 2014, there are certain classes of companies which are required to appoint Internal Auditors who shall either be a Chartered Accountant, Cost Accountant or such professional as may be decided by the Board to conduct internal audit of the company. The following companies will be required to keep internal auditor a) Listed company b) Private and unlisted public company if they meet following criteria:

Criteria	Private Company	Unlisted Public Company
Paid up share capital	No share capital	50 crores rupees or more during the preceding financial year

Turnover	200 crore rupees or more during the preceding financial year	200 crores rupees or more during the preceding financial year
Outstanding deposit	No deposit criteria	25 crore rupees or more at any point of time during the preceding financial year
Outstanding loans or borrowings	Exceeding 100 crores rupees or more at any given point during the preceding financial year	Exceeding 100 crores rupees or more at any given point during the preceding financial year

5.3.7 Reliance upon the work of Internal Auditor

SA-610 states that external auditor can use the work of internal auditor after evaluation of his work.

The external auditor needs to consider the following factors in determining the extent of reliance:

- Experience and qualification of internal audit
- The scope of internal audit report
- Whether internal audit is undertaken by separate outside agency
- Extent of authority vested on internal auditor
- Whether professional care has been taken by the internal auditor

It is thus to conclude that the external auditor can rely on the work of the internal auditor but his responsibility cannot be reduced due to reliance on the work of internal auditor and would be held responsible in case of any misstatements or negligence in his duty.

Chapter 6

Audit, Investigation and Forensic Audit

Introduction

Investigation is an in-depth examination of books of records for any specific purpose. It involves both financial and non-financial information. It refers to a planned, meticulous examination of books of accounts and transactions of an entity.

The actual aim of an investigation is to supply the client the required information in the form of a report about the matter specified.

An investigator may be appointed for the following purposes:

- An investigator may be appointed to find out the reasons for low profitability.
- He may be appointed to ascertain the nature of the fraud and the persons involved in fraudulent activities
- He may be appointed to check the creditworthiness of the prospective borrower
- He may be appointed to examine the rightness of such investment.
- He may be appointed to check the profitability and solvency position of the firm
- He may be appointed by the insurance company whether the claims are justified or not

- He may be appointed to examine the profitability and solvency of the firm to find the reasons of entering the new partnership firm does not backfire.
- Sometimes statutory investigation is required as per sections210, 212, 213 and 216 of the Companies Act 2013.

6.1 Features of investigation

The main features of investigation are:

i)Investigation is not compulsory and is conducted on voluntary basis.

ii)Investigation is for special purpose like financial position, earning capacity and fraud detection.

iii)The scope of the investigation is limited to questions asked in engagement letter.

iv)Investigations may be conducted for several years depending upon the requirement.

v)It is a thorough checking of book of accounts for a particular year.

vi)Investigation is free to design his plan of action as per requirements of the case.

6.2 Distinction between audit and investigation

S.No	Difference	Auditing	Investigation
1	Legal contract	Audit of annual financial statements is compulsory as per Companies Act 2013	Investigation is not compulsory
2	Time	Audit is conducted usually on an annual basis	It is conducted anytime for several years
3	Purpose	Aim is to ascertain whether financial statements show true and fair view	It is conducted to know specific object like financial position, earning capacity, invest capital etc
4	Person performing work	It is conducted by a professional expert like Chartered Accountant	It may be conducted by any person other than Chartered Accountant
5	Person for whom conducted	It is conducted on behalf of shareholders	It is conducted by outsiders such as buyers, investors etc
6	Evidence	It is usually concerned with	It is usually concerned with

		prima-facia evidence	conclusive evidence
7	Checking methods	Audit test checks are required	Thorough checking is required
8	Reporting	It is addressed to shareholders or proprietors	It is addressed to party on whose instructions investigations is carried on

Conclusion

An investigator is appointed to investigate any various purposes such as suspected fraud, to examine the nature and extent of sickness of an organisation, to judge the creditworthiness of the prospective borrower and to examine the reasons of unusual decline in profit etc. In such circumstances, the investigator has to draw the line of his course of action and proceed accordingly so that he can report to the appointing authority on time.

6.3 Forensic Audit

A forensic audit is a kind of investigation and examination of a company's financial records to derive evidence which can be used in a court of law or legal proceedings. It is conducted to prosecute a party for fraud, embezzlement or other financial claims. It is a specialization in the field of accounting and the audit covers a wide range of investigative activities performed by accountants.

6.3.1 Purpose of Forensic Audit

Forensic audit investigations are made for various reasons including the following:

i)Corruption

In Forensic Audit, an auditor would look for the following:

a)Conflict of interest

In case the fraudster uses his/her influence for personal gains detrimental to the company. To illustrate, A case whereas manager approves inaccurate expenses of an employee with whom he has personal relations. Even though he is not directly financially benefitted from this approval, it is deemed that he would receive personal benefits from such inappropriate approvals.

b)Bribery

It is a fraud where money is offered to get things done in one's favour. To illustrate, money being offered to a purchase manager to get the tender

c)Extortion

Extortion is when money is demanded in order to get the work done.

ii)Asset Misappropriation

It is the most common and prevalent form of fraud. Few examples of asset misappropriation are misappropriation of cash, raising fake invoices, misuse of assets, payments made to non-existing employees and misuse of assets or theft of inventory.

iii)Financial statement fraud

This kind of fraud is done by the company to try to show the company's financial performance better than what it actually is. The aim of presenting fraudulent numbers may be to improve liquidity or project market performance. Few examples of the financial statement fraud are the intentional forgery of accounting records, non-disclosure of relevant details from the financial statements or not applying the requisite financial reporting standards.

6.3.2 Procedure for a forensic audit investigation

A forensic auditor is required to have special training in forensic audit techniques as well as the legalities of accounting issues.

He has to perform the following steps in addition to regular audit procedures:

i)Plan the investigation

Firstly, the auditor is required to understand what the focus of the audit is. The auditor will plan their investigation to achieve objectives such as:

- Identify what fraud is being carried on
- Determine the time period during which the fraud is carried out
- Discover how the fraud was hidden
- Identify the perpetrators of the fraud
- Quantify the loss suffered

- Gather sufficient and relevant evidence which are admissible in the court
- Suggest measures those can prevent such frauds in the company

ii)Collecting Evidence

The auditor needs to understand the possible type of fraud that has been carried out and how it has been committed. The evidence collected should be adequate enough to prove the identify of the fraudsters in the court, reveal the details of fraud scheme and document the amount of loss.

A logical flow of evidence will help the court in understanding the fraud and the evidence presented. The auditor needs to ensure that the evidence are not altered or damaged by anyone.

Some common techniques used for collecting evidence in a forensic audit are:

- Substantive measures like doing a reconciliation or review of documents etc
- Analytical procedures used to compare trends over a certain period of time
- Computer assisted audit techniques like computer software programs that can be used to detect frauds
- Understanding internal controls and testing them to understand the loopholes due to which frauds happened
- Interviewing the culprits

iii)   Reporting

A report is required to be presented to the client about the fraud so that they can proceed to file a legal case. The report should contain the findings of the investigation, a summary of evidence, how fraud was committed and the suggestions on how internal controls can be improved to prevent such frauds in future.

iv)   Court Proceeding

The forensic auditor needs to be present during court proceedings to explain the evidence collected and how the suspect should be identified. They should simplify the complicated accounting language and explain in simple words for the people so that they can understand the fraud that was carried out.

Conclusion

A forensic audit is a detailed engagement which requires not only the expertise of accounting and auditing procedures but also knowledge of legal framework. He needs to have an understanding of all types of frauds and how evidences need to be collected.

Chapter 7

Company audit and other thrust areas

A company is a form of organisation which is created, maintained and terminated by the action of law. Every single event in a company is subject to certain legal provisions. Accordingly, auditing in a company is exclusively guided by the provisions of various acts, rules and other legal decisions. Hence, specific provisions covering all relevant aspects of audit and auditor have been incorporated to attain highest possible standards.

7.1 Qualifications of a Company Auditor

Every company is required to undergo statutory audit by a statutory auditor. The following persons can be considered as qualified for this purpose as per section 141 of Companies Act, 2013:

- If he is a Chartered Accountant
- A firm can also be appointed as an auditor if majority of partners practising in India qualifies as company auditor
- When a firm including a limited liability partnership is appointed as an auditor of a company, only the partners who are Chartered Accountants shall be authorised to act and sign on behalf of the firm

7.2 Disqualification of a company Auditor

The following persons shall not be eligible for appointment as an auditor of a company:

i)A body corporate other than a limited liability partnership registered under the Limited Liability Partnership Act 2008.

ii)An officer or employee of the company

iii)A person who is a partner, or who is in the employment of an officer or employee of the company

iv)A person who is a relative or partner

v)A person or a firm who directly or indirectly has business relationship with the company

vi) a person whose relative is a director or in the employment of a company as director or key managerial personnel.

vii)A person who is in full employment elsewhere or a person or partner holding appointment as an auditor is such persons or partner is at the time of such appointment or reappointment holding appointment as auditor of more than twenty companies

viii)A person who has been convicted by a court of an offence involving fraud and a period of ten years has not elapsed from the date of such conviction

ix)Any person whose subsidiary or associate company is engaged as on the date of appointment in consulting and specialised services as provided in section 144

7.3 Ceiling on the number of audit

As per section 141 (3) (g), a person or a partner of a firm shall not be eligible for appointment as the auditor of a company if :

i)Such person is in full time employment elsewhere

ii)Such person or partner is at the date of such appointment or reappointment, holding appointment as auditor of more than twenty companies excluding private limited companies, dormant, small companies and One Person Companies.

7.4 Rights of auditor of a company

Every auditor needs certain rights and powers in order to discharge his duties effectively. The rights area as follows:

- Right to inspect books of accounts and vouchers
- Right to obtain information and explanations
- Right to inspect branch offices and branch accounts
- Right to receive the report of branch audit from the branch auditor
- Right to receive notices and attend general meetings
- Right to sign the audit report and other documents
- Right to have audit report read at the AGM
- Right to attend the meeting of the audit committee
- Right to take legal and technical advice
- Right to claim remuneration

7.5 Duties of a company auditor

The Companies Act 2013 contains comprehensive provisions regarding the duties of a company auditor. They are:

- Duty to make enquiry
- Duty to prepare and submit report on financial statements
- Duty to comply with the directions of CAG
- Duty to comply with auditing standards
- Duty to give reasons for any negative remarks qualification
- Duty to report any fraud to the Central Government
- Duty of Cost Accountant and Company Secretary regarding audit
- Duty to pay penalty
- Duty to make comments sought by the audit committee on certain matters

7.6 Branch Audit

Every company shall prepare and keep at its registered office books of accounts and other relevant books and financial statements for every financial year which give true and fair view of the state of the affairs of the company including that of its branch office or offices. The books at both the registered office and its branches shall be kept on accrual basis and according to the double entry system.

According to Section 143 (8) of the Companies Act 2013, the provisions of the accounts of a branch office of a company should be kept as follows:

i)Where a company has a branch office, the accounts of that office shall be audited either by the auditor appointed for the company under this Act or by any other person qualified for appointment as an auditor of the company under this Act and appointed as such under Section 139

ii)Where the branch office is situated outside India, the accounts of the branch office shall be audited either by the company's auditor or by any person duly qualified as an auditor in accordance with the laws of the country

iii)If the branch auditor is appointed separately, the duties and powers of the branch auditor shall be same as applicable to the company auditor.

iv)The branch auditor shall prepare a report on the accounts of the branch examined by him and send it to the auditor of the company who shall deal with it in his report in the manner necessary.

v)Section 143(12) regarding reporting of fraud by the auditor shall also extend to the branch auditor to the extent it relates to the concerned branch.

7.7 Joint Audit

Joint audit refers to the system of appointing more than one audit firm or individual chartered accountants to conduct the audit of a single organisation. Large companies prefer to keep joint auditors to ensure pooling together the resources and expertise of multiple auditors to perform the audit efficiently and within a given period of time.

Benefits of Joint Audit

i)It helps pooling of expertise of more than one auditor

ii)The workload of each individual auditor is reduced

iii)It ensures better quality of performance

iv)It enhances the effectiveness of the audit work

v)In case of multinational companies with subsidiaries in different countries, joint auditor can spread the work using the expertise of local firms which are in a better position to deal with local laws and regulations

Limitations of Joint audit

The general limitations of joint audit are;

i)Lack of proper co-ordination among the auditors is a problem.

ii) There may be confusion with regard to the responsibility of each auditor.

iii)Superiority complex o few auditors can cause conflict

iv)Uncertainty may arise as regards to the liability of any work done.

v)Disagreement among the joint auditors may cause delay in finalisation of audit report.

7.7.1 Regulatory Guidelines in respect of Joint Audit

SA 299 on 'Responsibility of Joint Auditor' has given the following guidelines in respect with joint audit of companies.

A. Division of Audit Work

- The joint auditors should divide the audit work among themselves through mutual discussion or on the basis of identifiable units or specified areas. In case it is not possible, the division of work may be with reference to items of assets or liabilities or income or expenditure or with reference to periods of time.
- Certain areas of work will not be divided and will be covered by all the joint auditors
- The division of work among joint auditors should be well documented and preferably communicated to the entity.

B. Co-ordination and responsibility of a Joint Auditor

The joint auditors must co-ordinate amongst themselves in course of audit work. In case a joint auditor comes across matters of relevance to the areas of responsibility of other joint auditors, he should communicate the same to all the joint auditors in writing in the form of a report.

Otherwise, each joint auditor is responsible only for the work allocated to him. So, among other duties:

Each joint auditor needs to scrutinise the audit report of the branches specifically allocated to him and obtain and evaluate information and explanations of units allocated to him.

However, they should be jointly and severally responsible for the following:

- In respect of undivided work

- In respect of decisions taken jointly regarding the nature, timing or extent of audit procedures to be performed by any of the joint auditor.
- In respect of matters which are brought to the notice of the joint auditors by any one of them and on which there is no agreement among them.
- With regards to compliance with disclosure requirement of the relevant statue in the financial statements
- To ensure that the audit report complies with the requirements of the relevant statue.

C. Reliance on the work of other joint auditor

Each joint auditor is entitled to rely on the other joint auditors for bringing to his notice any departure from the generally accepted accounting principles or any material error noticed in the course of audit.

D. Reporting responsibility

Generally, the joint auditors are able to submit a unanimous audit report. However, in case of disagreement, each of them can express his own opinion through a separate report. A joint auditor is not bound by the views of the majority of them.

7.8 Related Party Disclosures as per SA 550

Few transactions are entered into between a company and its officials as a party related to any such officials during the course of the business. It is possible that these transactions do not necessarily indicate any fraudulent intentions, yet they may at times indicate any material misstatement leading to distortion of financial state of affairs of a company. Hence, an auditor needs to be extra cautious while dealing with such relationships and follow all regulatory guidelines.

SA 550 on 'Related Parties' provide extensive guidelines relating to transactions with related parties and auditors' duty thereon. These are as follows:

A. Nature of related party transactions

Many related party transactions are in the normal course of business and do not carry higher risk of material mis-statement. However, it is possible that a few transactions may give rise to high risk of material mis-statement, especially when the related parties operate through a complex range of relationships, the information is ineffective at identifying or summarising transactions and the transactions are conducted other than the normal course of business.

B. Auditor's Responsibility

It will be the duty of the auditor to perform audit procedure to identify, assess and respond to the risk of material misstatement coming from the failure of the organisation to account for or disclose such relationships and transactions. It is the duty of the auditor to obtain an understanding of such relationships and transactions to be able to conclude that the financial statements are true and fair and are not misleading.

C. Aim of the auditor

The aim of the auditor will be:

i)To obtain an understanding of such relationship and transactions to be able to recognise fraud risk factor and conclude that the financial statements are true and fair and are not misleading

ii)To obtain appropriate and sufficient audit evidence about whether such relationships have been properly identified, accounted for and disclosed

D. Risk Assessment Procedure to be followed

The auditor must follow following risk assessment procedures:

i) Understanding the entity's related party relationships and transactions

ii) Maintaining alertness for related party information when reviewing records or documents

iii) Sharing related party information with the engagement team

E. Identification and assessment of the risks of material misstatements

- The author needs to identify and assess the risk of material misstatement associated with related party relationships and transactions and ascertain whether such risks are of importance
- The auditor shall design and perform further audit procedures to obtain sufficient and appropriate audit evidence related to risk of material misstatement
- The auditor identifies previously unidentified and undisclosed relationships and significant transactions and shall promptly communicate the relevant information to the other members of the engagement team
- He further performs appropriate substantive procedures related to newly identified related parties

- He re-considers the risks and evaluates the implication for the same.
- The auditor shall obtain appropriate audit evidence about the assertion by management regarding conduct of related party transaction
- The auditor shall evaluate the identified related party transactions and see if they are accounted for and disclosed in accordance with the applicable reporting framework.

F. Written representations

The auditor shall obtain written representation from the management and those charged with governance about the entity's related parties and all their related party relationships and ensure they are properly accounted for and disclosed.

7.9 Written representation by management

SA 580 'Written Representation' provides guidelines with regards to written representation to be obtained by the auditor from the management during the course of audit work. It is a written statement by management given to the auditor to support other audit evidence and other matters. However, this does not include financial statements etc.

Written representations are kind of audit evidence only as they give necessary information that the auditor requires in connection with financial statements. They however are not sufficient audit evidence on their own.

7.9.1 Auditor's aim in obtaining written representation

The aim of the auditor are:

- To obtain written representation from the management that they have fulfilled the responsibility for the preparation of the financial statements
- To support other audit evidence relevant to the financial statements
- To respond appropriately in case the management do not provide the written representation.

7.9.2 Auditor's duty regarding written management

An auditor's duty with regards to written representation is as follows:

A. Extent of reliability of written representation

In case written representations are inconsistent with other audit evidence and the auditor has concerns about the competence of management, then he shall perform audit procedures to resolve the matter. In case the matter remains unresolved, the auditor shall reconsider the assessment of the management and shall determine its effect on the reliability of oral and written representations and audit evidence in general.

The auditor shall take appropriate actions if he concludes that the written representations are not reliable.

B. Requested written representations not provided

In case the management does not provide one or more of the requested written representations, the auditor shall:

- Discuss the matter with the management
- Re-evaluate the integrity of the management
- Take appropriate actions including determining the possible effects on the opinion in the auditor's report.

C. Disclaimer of opinion

The auditor shall disclaim an opinion on the financial statements if:

- The auditor has sufficient doubt on the integrity of the management and the written representations are not reliable
- Management does not give the required written representations.

Chapter 8

Auditing Standards

Introduction

There has been a growth in global trade during the last few years. There has been a highly competitive, expanding economy, explosive use of technology, increase in public entities and unprecedented growth in the market value of these securities. Keeping this in mind, the professional accountants have adhered to standards and procedures laid down by the professional accountancy bodies.

In simple language, auditing standards show a modification in the best practice of the profession. Auditing standards helps in optimum and proper discharge of their professional duties. It also promotes uniformity in practice as also responsibility.

8.1 Importance of Standards on Auditing

The SA give general guidelines and techniques of auditing to be followed by the auditors in different audit environment. The importance of the SA is follows:

- The objective of issuing these guidelines is to ensure sound and effective auditing practices.
- These guidelines attempt to codify the auditing practices to be applied while conducting an audit

- Auditing, not being a very exact science, needed auditing standards to bring uniformity in the concepts, conventions and practices
- Standardisation of auditing terminology is necessary to prevent misuse of auditing terminology and prevent accounting scandals

8.2 Engagement and Quality Standards

The International Federation of Accountants 9IFAC) set up the International Auditing and Assurance Standards Board.

The Institute of Chartered Accountants of India (ICAI) , being a member of IFAC, also set-up the Auditing and assistance Standards Board in July 2002

i)To review the existing auditing practices in India

ii)To develop statements on Engagement and Quality Control Standards

It will apply whenever an independent financial audit is carried out.

8.3 Procedure for application

- The Auditing and Assurance Standards Board (AASB) determines the area in which the Engagement and Quality Standards need to be formulated.
- The AASB is assisted by study groups constituted to consider specific subjects and provision is made for participation of a cross section of members of the institute.

- An exposure draft of the proposed Engagement and Quality Control Standards is prepared by the board and is issued for comments by members of the Institute
- Henceforth, the draft is finalised and submitted to the council of the institute
- The council will consider the final draft and if necessary, modify the same.

8.4 Purpose of the Auditing Standards

- The title of the Preface issued by the Council of the Institute of Chartered Accountants of India is "Preface to the Standards on Quality Control, auditing Review, Other Assurance and Related Services."
- The preface has been issued to help in the understanding of the scope and authority of the pronouncements of the AASB.
- The ICAI is committed to provide the services of high quality in the public interest and also develops and promulgates technical standards and other things in order to achieve the goal.
- The Indian Standards promulgated to confirm to the International Standards issued by the International Auditing and Assurance Standards Board.

8.5 Standard on Quality Control (SQC) 1

Quality Control for firms that perform audits and reviews of historical financial information and other assurance and related services engagements

Introduction

The firm should establish a system of quality control designed to provide it with reasonable assurance that the firm and its personnel comply with professional standards and legal requirements.

Elements of a System on Quality Control

The firm system of quality control should include policies and procedures on the following elements:

- Leadership responsibilities for quality within the firm
- Ethical requirements
- Acceptance and continuance of client relationships and specific engagements
- Human resources
- Engagement performance
- Monitoring

Let us study in detail.

i)Leadership Responsibilities for Quality

It is necessary that the policies and procedures should be designed to promote an internal culture that quality is essential in performing engagements. The system should be such that the firm's highest authority is to assume ultimate responsibility for the system of quality control. Any person or persons assigned responsibility for quality control system should have sufficient and appropriate experience, ability and the necessary authority.

ii)Ethical Requirements

The policies and procedures should be such that all concerned personnel comply with relevant ethical requirements. Policies and procedures should emphasise the basic principles:

- Leadership of the firm
- Monitoring
- Education and training
- A process for dealing with non-compliance

iii)Independence

The policies and procedures should be such that all concerned should maintain independence where required by the Code. It should enable the firm to:

- Communicate its independent requirements
- Identify circumstances that create threats to independence and to take appropriate action to eliminate or reduce threats to an acceptable level by applying safeguards or if appropriate should withdraw from the engagement.

Such policies and procedures should require:

i)Personnel to provide the firm with relevant information about client's engagement, the scope of services and to evaluate the impact on independence requirements

ii)Personnel to promptly notify circumstances that create a threat to independence for taking appropriate action iii)Accumulate and communicate relevant information to appropriate personnel so that:

- All can readily determine satisfaction of independence requirements
- Maintain and update records relating to independence
- Take appropriate action regarding identified threats to
  a)All to promptly notify on becoming aware about the breaches of independence

  b)All to promptly communicate breaches of these policies and procedures to the one who needs to address the breach and those who need to take appropriate action

  c)The firm should obtain written communication of compliance with its policies and procedures on independence annually

  d) Setting out criteria for determining the safeguards to reduce the familiarity threat to an acceptable level over a long period of time

iv)**Acceptance and Continuance of client relationships and specific Engagements**

Policies and procedures for the acceptance and continuance of client relationships and specific engagements should be so designed to provide it with reasonable assurance to undertake or continue relationships and engagements only where it:

- Has considered the integrity of the client
- Is competent capable and has time and resources to do so

- Can comply with the ethical requirements and it should document how the issues regarding ethical requirements were resolved

v)Human Resources

Policies and procedures should be so designed to provide with reasonable assurance that it has sufficient personnel with the capabilities, competence and commitment to ethical principles necessary to perform its engagements in accordance with professional standards and to enable all to issue reports that are appropriate in the circumstances.

The firm should assign responsibility for each assignment to an engagement partner with policies and procedures requiring that:

- The identity and role of the engagement partner are communicated to key members of the client's management and those charged with governance
- The responsibilities of the engagement partner are clearly defined and communicated to that partner

vi)Engagement Performance

Policies and procedures should be designed in such a way to provide with reasonable assurance that engagements are performed in accordance with professional standards and regulatory and legal requirements.

The policies and procedures are designed to provide with reasonable assurance that:

- Appropriate consultation takes place on difficult or contentious matters

- Sufficient resources are available to enable appropriate consultation
- The nature and scope of consultations are documented
- Conclusions from consultations are documented and implemented

In case of policies and procedures for dealing with and resolving difference of opinion within the engagement team, then the conclusions thereon should be documented and implemented.

8.5.1 Engagement Quality Control Review

- Need of an engagement quality control review for all audits of financial statements of listed entities
- Set out criteria against which all other audits and reviews of historical financial information and other assurance should be evaluated to determine whether an engagement quality control review should be performed
- Policies and procedures setting out the nature, timing and extent of an engagement quality control review. The policies should address the appointment of engagement quality control reviewers and establish their eligibility through the technical qualifications, experience and authority
- Documentation requirements for an engagement quality control review

8.5.2 Engagement documentation

Policies and procedure on documentation of the engagement quality control review should ensure that

- The procedures related to quality control reviewer have been performed
- The quality control review completed before the report is issued
- The reviewer is not aware of any unresolved matters about inappropriate conclusions

There should be policies and procedures for engagement teams to complete the assembly of final engagement files on a timely basis after the engagement reports have been finalised. The policies and procedures should be so designed to maintain the confidentiality, safe custody, integrity, accessibility and retrievability of engagement documentation. The engagement documents should be retained for a period sufficient to meet the needs of the firm or as required by law or regulation, which should not be shorter than 7 years from the date of report.

8.5.3 Ownership of Engagement Documentation and monitoring

The policies and procedures relating to the system of quality control are relevant, adequate, operating effectively and complied with in practice. Such policies and procedures should include an outgoing consideration and evaluation of the firm's system of quality control including a periodic inspection of a selection of completed engagements.

The deficiencies found in monitoring process and the recommendations for appropriate remedial actions should be communicated to relevant engagement partners. Firm should determine what further action is required to comply with relevant professional standards and legal requirements including obtaining legal advice.

8.5.4 Complaints and Allegations

The policies and procedures should be such those provide with reasonable assurance:

- Complaints and allegations that the work performed by the firm fails to comply with professional standards and regulatory and legal
- Allegations of non-compliance with the firm's system of quality control

Chapter 9

Engagement Standards

9.1 Meaning and types

The Standards issued by the Auditing and Assurance Standards Board under the authority of the Council are known as Engagement Standards.

The different types of engagement standards:

i)   **Standards on Auditing (SAs)** are to be applied in the audit of historical financial information.

ii) **Standards on Review Engagements (SREs)** are to be applied in the review of historical financial information.

iii) **Standards on Assurance Engagements (SAEs)** are to be applied in assurance dealing with matters other than historical financial information.

iv) **Standards on Related Services (SRSs)** are applied to engagements related to compilation agreements and other related services.

9.2 Standards on Auditing

The Standards on Auditing are formulated in the context of an audit of financial statements by an independent auditor. It has to be adapted when applied to audit of other financial information.

9.2.1 Objectives of Audit

- The aim of a financial audit is to enable the auditor to express an opinion whether the financial statements are prepared in all material aspects. It helps to enhance the degree of confidence of intended users in the financial statements.
- The auditor needs to ascertain whether the financial statements are free of material misstatements.
- There is a chance that there is an unavoidable risk that some material misstatements of the financial statements will not be detected owing to the inherent limitations of an audit.
- When the auditor is not able to achieve overall objective, the SA require the auditor to modify the auditor's opinion or withdraw from the engagement.

9.2.2 Requirements

- The requirements of each SA are contained in a separate section and are expressed using shall.
- The auditor applies the requirements in the context of other material included in the Standard
- The auditor complies with the requirements of SA in all cases where they are relevant in the circumstances of the audit.
- The auditor may depart from a relevant requirement when:
  i)The requirement is for a specific procedure to be performed and
  ii)The procedure is ineffective in the specific circumstances of the audit

- The auditor is required to document the following:
  i)How alternative procedures performed achieve the aim of the requirement
  ii)The reasons for the departure
- Auditors report should draw attention to such departures. However, a mere disclosure in the report does not absolve him from complying with the applicable Standards
- A requirement is not relevant only in the cases where the SA is not relevant or the circumstances do not apply because the requirement is conditional and the condition does not exist.
- The auditor is not required to comply with the irrelevant circumstances of the audit. However, the auditor needs to document the same.

9.2.3 Audits and Reviews of Historical and Financial Information

a)100-999 Standards on Auditing (SAs)

i)100-199 introductory Matters

ii)200-299 General Principles and Responsibilities

iii)SA 200 (AAS-1), Basic Principles Governing an Audit

iv)SA200A (AAS-2), Objective and Scope of the Audit of Financial Statements

v)SA210 (AAS-26) Terms of Audit Engagement

vi) SA 220 (AAS-17) Quality Control for Audit Work

vii)SA 230 (AAS-3) Documentation

viii)SA 240 (AAS-4) The Auditor's Responsibility to Consider Fraud and Error in an Audit of Financial Statement

ix)SA240 (Revised) under the Clarity Project, The Auditor's Responsibilities Relating to Fraud in the Audit of Financial Statements

x)SA 250 (AAS-21) Consideration of Laws and Regulation in an Audit of Financial Statements

xi)SA250 (Revised) under the Clarity Project, Consideration of Laws and Regulations in an audit of Financial Statements

xii)SA 260 (AAS-27), Communication of Audit Matters with those charged with Governance

xiii) SA 299 (AAs-12), Responsibility of Joint Auditors

b) 300-499 Risk assessment and response to assessed risks

i)SA 300 (AAs-8) Audit Planning

ii) SA 300 (Revised) under the Clarity Project, Planning an Audit of Financial Statements

iii)SA 300 (AAS-20), Knowledge of the Business

iv)SA 315 under the Clarity Project, identifying and assessing the Risks of Material Misstatement through Understanding the Entity and its Environment

v)SA 320 (AAS-13) Audit Materiality

vi) SA 330 under the Clarity Project, the Auditor's Response to Assessed Risks

vii)SA 400 (AAS-6) Risk Assessments and Internal Control

viii)SA 401 (AAS-29), audit in a Computer Information Systems Environment

ix)SA 402 (AAS-24), Audit Considerations Relating to Entities Using Service Organisations

c)500-599 Audit Evidence

i) SA 500 (AAS-5), audit Evidence

ii)SA 501 (AAS-34), Audit Evidence-Additional Considerations for Specific Items

iii)SA505 (AAS-30), External Confirmations

iv)SA 510 (AAS-22) Initial Engagements- Opening Balance

v)SA520 (AAS-14), Analytical Procedures

vi)SA 530 (AAS-15), Audit Sampling

vii)SA540 (AAS-18), Auditing of Accounting Estimates

viii)SA 550 (AAS-23) Related Parties

ix)SA560 (AAS-19) Subsequent Events

x)SA 570 (AAS-16) Going Concern

xi)SA 580 (AAS-11), Representations by Management

xii)SA 580 (revised) under the Clarity Project, Written Representations

d) 600-699 Using work of others

i)SA 600 (AAs-10), Using the Work of Another Auditor

ii)SA610(AAS-7), Relying Upon the Work of an Internal auditor

iii)SA620 (AAS-9), Using the work of an Expert

e) 700-799 Audit conclusions and reporting

i)SA700 (AAS-28), The Auditor's Report on Financial Statements

ii) SA 710 (AAS-25), Comparatives

f) 800-899 specialised areas

9.3 Standards on Review Engagements

Standards on Review Engagements establish requirements and provide application and other explanatory material on the responsibilities of an auditor if he is engaged to undertake a review engagement and on the form and content of the auditors and their review report.

The standard that deals with review engagements are:

2000-2699 Standards on Review Engagements (SREs)

SRE 2400 (AAS-33), Engagements to Review Financial Statements

9.4 Assurance Engagements other than audits or review of historical financial information

The Framework for Assurance Engagements deals with assurance engagements performed by auditors. It provides a frame of reference for practitioners with assurance engagements. It also identifies the aims of the two types of assurance engagements

i)   Reasonable assurance engagements

ii)   Limited assurance engagements

9.4.1 Definition and Objective of an assurance Engagement

Assurance Engagement is an engagement in which a practitioner expresses a conclusion aimed to enhance the degree of confidence for the intended users about the outcome of the evaluation or measurement of a subject matter against criteria.

Subject matter information fails to be properly expressed in the context of the subject matter and the criteria and so can be misstated to a material extent. This occurs when the subject matter information does not properly reflect the application of the subject matter criteria To illustrate, when an entity's financial statements do not give a true and fair view of its financial statements or when an entity's assertion that its internal control is effective is not fairly stated in all material aspects.

9.4.2 Assertion based vs Direct Reporting Engagements

An assertion based engagement is when the evaluation or measurement of the subject matter is performed by the responsible party and the subject matter is in the form of an assertion by the responsible party that is made available to the intended users.

In Direct Reporting engagement, the practitioner either directly performs the evaluation of the subject matter or obtains a representation from the responsible party that has performed the evaluation that is not available to the intended users. The subject matter is provided to the intended users in the assurance report.

9.4.3 Reasonable vs Limited Engagements

The objective of a reasonable engagement is a reduction in assurance engagement risk to an acceptably low level in the circumstance of the engagement as the basis for a positive form of expression.

The aim of a limited assurance engagement is a reduction in assurance engagement risk to a level that is acceptable in the circumstance of the engagement, but where that risk is greater than for a reasonable assurance engagement, as a basis for a negative form of expression.

9.4.4 Elements of an Assurance Engagement

The following are the five elements of an assurance engagement:

i)Three party relationship

There are three separate parties in an assurance engagement:

A practitioner is broader than the term auditor as used in SAs and SREs, which relates only to practitioners performing audit or review engagements with respect to historical financial information.

The responsible party is the person who is responsible for the subject matter in a direct reporting engagement and is responsible for the subject matter information and the subject matter in an assertion based engagement.

The intended users are the person or persons for whom the practitioner prepares the assurance report. The responsible party can be one of the intended users but not the only one.

ii)Subject matter and Subject Matter Information

The subject matter and subject matter information of an assurance engagement can take different forms:

a)Financial performance such as financial or prospective financial position and cash flows for which subject matter is recognition, measurement, presentation and disclosure shown in financial statements.

b) Non-financial performance such as performance of an entity for which the subject matter may be key indicators of efficiency and effectiveness

c) Systems and processes such as internal control for which subject matter is assertion about effectiveness

d) Physical characteristics such as capacity of a facility for which the subject matter is specifications document

e) Behaviour such as corporate governance, compliance with regulation, human resource practices for which subject matter is a statement of compliance or effectiveness

iii) Criteria

Criteria are the benchmarks used to evaluate or measure the subject matter such as benchmark for presentation and disclosure. Criteria may be formal such as in preparation of financial statements, the criteria may be Accounting Standards. Criteria may be less formal such as an internally developed code of conduct or an agreed level of performance.

iv) Evidence

a) The practitioner takes into consideration materiality, assurance engagement risk and the quantity and quality of available evidence when planning and performing the engagement when determining the nature, timing and extent of evidence gathering information.

b) The practitioner uses his professional scepticism to make a critical assessment.

c) The evidence is required to be sufficient and appropriate.

d) It is required of the practitioner to obtain sufficient appropriate evidence to be able to be in a position to express a conclusion in the positive form required in a reasonable assurance engagement. To be able to achieve the above, the practitioner needs to:

- Obtain an understanding of the subject matter
- Assess the risk that the subject matter information may be materially misstated
- Develop overall responses and determining the nature, timing and extent of further procedures

- Use a combination of inspection, observation, confirmation, re-calculation, re-performance, analytical procedures and inquiry

v)Absolute assurance

Reasonable assurance is less than absolute assurance. Reducing assurance engagement risk to zero is very rarely possible due to following factors:

- Use of selective testing
- Inherent limitations of internal control
- Evidence available is persuasive rather than conclusive
- Use of judgement in gathering and evaluating evidence and thereby forming conclusion

9.4.5 Assurance Report

a) Written report

The practitioner gives a written report containing a conclusion that conveys the assurance obtained about the subject matter. SAs, SREs and SAEs establish basic element for assurance reports.

b) Assertion based engagement report

In an assertion-based engagement, the practitioner's conclusion can be worked either in terms of the responsible party's assertion or directly in terms of the subject matter and the criteria.

c) Direct reporting engagement report

In a direct reporting engagement, the practitioner's conclusion is worded directly in terms of the subject matter and the criteria.

d)**Reasonable assurance engagement report**

In a reasonable assurance engagement, the practitioner expresses the conclusion in the positive form such as "In our opinion control is effective, in all material aspects, based on ABC criteria."

e)**Limited assurance report**

In a limited assurance engagement, the practitioner expresses the conclusion in the negative form such as "based on our work as in the report, nothing has come to our attention that causes us to believe that internal control is not effective, in all material effects, based on ABC criteria".

The standards those deal with the assurance engagements are:

a)3000-3699 Standards on assurance Engagements (SAEs)

b)3000-3399 Applicable to all Assurance Engagements

c)3400 -3699 Subject Specific Standards

d)SAE 3400 (AAS-35), The Examination of Prospective Financial Information

9.5 Standards on Related Services(SRSs)

Standards on Related Services establish requirements and provide application and other explanatory material on the responsibilities of an assurance practitioner, when engaged to undertake engagements.

The aim of this standard is to provide standards and guidance on the professional responsibilities of an auditor when the engagement for performing agreed-upon procedures concerning financial information is assumed. The agreed upon procedures engagement requires an auditor to execute procedures of the audit nature to which the entity, the auditor and the third parties have decided to report on the actual findings. The auditor does not give any assurance in his report since he basically offers a report of factual findings of the agreed-upon procedures.

9.5.1 General principles of an agreed-upon procedures engagement

An auditor should adhere to the Code of Ethics issued by ICAI. Ethical principles which govern the professional responsibilities of the auditor are:

- Integrity
- Confidentiality
- Due care
- Professional competence
- Objectivity
- Technical Standards
- Professional conduct

In case the auditor is not independent, he must provide a statement to such effect in his report.

9.5.2 Planning and Documentation

An auditor must plan his work in a manner that the engagement is executed efficiently. He needs to document all crucial matters and help him to provide evidence in support of his report of factual findings.

9.5.3 Procedures and Evidence

The procedures used by an auditor in an engagement to perform agreed-upon procedures include:

- Enquiry and analysis
- Observation
- Inspection
- Comparison, re-computation and other tests
- Obtaining confirmations

The standards those deal with standards on related services are:

a)4000-4699 Standards on Related Services (SRSs)

- SRS 4400 (AAS-32), Engagements to perform Agreed-Upon Procedures Regarding Financial information
- SRS 440 (AAS-31), Engagements to Compile Financial information

Chapter 10

Audit report and certificates

Introduction

An audit report is a document of collected facts and written in standard format through which the auditor expresses his opinion regarding the reliability and accuracy of the financial statements of the organisation. It is the final work of an audit. The concept of materiality plays a crucial role in forming an opinion of the auditor about the true and fair view of financial statements.

10.1 Characteristics of a good audit report

The following are the features of a good audit report:

- A good audit report should be simple and easy to understand.
- The report should be clear and unambiguous.
- It should be concise, accurate and specific. It means that a good audit report should transmit maximum information in minimum words.
- Consistency in presenting accounting information should be maintained throughout the report.

- It should disclose all facts and truth. It is essential that all relevant matters should be properly disclosed as per the regulations.
- It should clearly state the scope of work done.
- It should be based on objective evidence i.e.it should facilitate comparison of financial statements with reliability and uniformity.
- The recommendations made at the end of the report should be unbiased and impartial.
- A report should be prepared and presented within stipulated time.
- Relevant and accurate information should be included in the report.

10.2 Importance of audit report

An audit report is of immense use to the following parties:

i) **Shareholders:** Audit report helps shareholders in understanding how the company is progressing and whether the money they have invested is properly used or no.

ii) **Investors:** Investors use audit report to assess the risk of the company before making any decision.

iii) **Financing and Lending Institutions:** Banks and lending institutions assess the credit worthiness, liquidity position and profitability of the company as per audit report

iv) **Insurance Claim:** An audit report helps in expediting the process of settlement from the insurance company

v) Mergers: Potential merger partners use audit report to evaluate a company before taking the decision of merger.

vi) Suppliers: Suppliers look upto the audit report to know the paying capacity of the company

vii) Insolvency: Audit report forms a basis of determining the action based on insolvency and bankruptcy.

viii) Decision making: The auditor's report is considered for taking many decisions.

10.3 Requirements of a good audit report

As per SA-700 "Forming an opiinion and reporting on Financial Statements", the requirements and basic elements of good audit report are:

i)An audit report should have appropriate title like " **Auditor's Report**"

ii)The Auditor's Report should be addressed as required by the circumstances of the situation. It should be addressed to the shareholders in case of the company and to the proprietor, partners etc in other cases.

iii)The introductory paragraph of the auditor's report shall state that the financial statements have been audited and

- specify the entity whose financial statements have been audited
- specify the title of each statement that comprises financial statement

- make reference to the summary of significant accounting policies and information
- specify the date and period covered by each statement.

iv)A section with the heading of **'Management's Responsibilities for the Financial Statements'** has to be included in the Auditor's Report. In this section, the report should state that the financial statements are basically the responsibility of the management.

v)A section with heading **"Auditor's Responsibility"** has to be included in the Auditor's report. The audit report shall state that the responsibility of the auditor is to express an opinion on the financial statements based on the audit.

vi)Further, a section with the heading **'Opinion'** has to be included in the auditor's report. The auditor needs to give opinion that the financial statements give a true and fair view.

vii)Sometimes, a separate section having the subtitle **'Report on other legal and Regulatory Requirements'** has to be included in the Auditor's Report.

viii)The audit report should clearly identify the financial statements e.g. the balance sheet and profit and loss account of ABC Company Limited for the year ended 31.3.200....

ix)The Auditor's Report has to be signed in personal name and in the name of the audit firm as well. The partner or the proprietor signing the report has to mention the **'Firm Registration Number'** and **'Membership Number'** assigned by the Institute of Chartered Accountants.

x)The date of the Auditor's Report is the date on which the auditor signs the report expressing his opinion on the financial statement.

xi)The auditor's report shall name the place of the specific location where the report is signed.

10.4 Format od Audit Report

SA 700 contain the following example of a complete audit report showing the basic elements of a report

---

Auditor's Report

We have audited the attached balance sheet of .... name of the entity) as at 31st March 2XXX and also the profit and loss account for the year ended on that date annexed therein.

These financial statements are the responsibility of the management of the company. Our responsibility is to express an opinion on these financial statements based on audit.

We conducted our audit in accordance with auditing standards generally accepted in India. Those standards require that we plan and perform the audit to obtain reasonable assurance whether the financial statements are free of material misstatements. We believe that our audit provides a reasonable basis for our opinion.

In our opinion and to the best of our information given to us, the financial statements give a true and fair view in conformity with the accounting principles generally accepted in India.

---

i)In the case of the balance sheet of the state of affairs of
..........(name of the entity) as at 31st march 2XXX, and

ii)In the case of the profit and loss account, of the profit/loss
for the year ended on the date.

For XYZ and Co
Chartered Accountants
Auditor's signature
(Name of member signing the audit report)
(Designation)
(Membership Number)
Place of signature
Date

10.5 Types of Audit Report

The audit report may be of two types:

a)Unmodified Audit Report

b))Modified or clean audit report

a)Unmodified or Clean Audit Report

The Auditor submits an unmodified report when he does not
have any reservation with regards to the matters in the financial
statements. Here, the auditor states that the financial statements
give a true and fair view of the state of affairs for the period.

An unqualified opinion states that

i)The financial statements are prepared using the generally accepted accounting principles which have been consistently applied

ii)The financial statements comply with relevant statutory requirements and regulations

iii)There is adequate disclosure of all material matters and proper presentation of financial information

b)**Modified Audit Report**

Any audit report other than an unqualified report is known as modified report as per SA700. An auditor's report may be modified by including a paragraph drawing attention to a particular matter. Such matter may be explained in detail in the notes in accounts.

Such paragraph modifies the standard format of audit report but it does not affect the unqualified opinion. Such paragraph should be placed before the opinion paragraph in the report and should specifically mention that the auditor's opinion is nor qualified in this regard.

For example. "Without qualifying our opinion, we draw attention to Note 8 of schedule .... To the financial statements that the company is defending a legal case claiming damage for infringement of patterns. The present liability is unknown and no provision is made."

 A modified audit report may be the following types:

i)Qualified audit report

ii)Adverse audit report

iii)Audit report with disclaimer of opinion

iv)Piecemeal audit report

i)Qualified Audit Report

When the auditor gives an opinion subject to reservations, it is said to be a Qualified Audit Report. It is to be noted that the auditor is dissatisfied regarding some matters and not all matters. Also the matters are not that important to make the accounts unreliable.

Few situations leading to the qualified report are:

- Non adherence to AS-2 regarding inventory valuation at the lower of cost and realisable value
- Auditor not allowed to observe the counting of physical inventory

The auditor may report that "subject to such matters......I report that....the accounts give true and fair view......"

ii)Adverse Audit Report

When an auditor gives a negative opinion or is not satisfied regarding any or some of the vital matters, then it is said to be adverse report. The matters are so essential to make the accounts unreliable and will affect the true or fair view of the accounts.

Few situations leading to an adverse opinion are:

- Serious misappropriation of funds committed by the management
- The company has failed to make provisions of bad debts to about 40 percent

The report would say that "In view of so and so matters......the accounts do not give a true and fair view......."

iii)Audit Report with Disclaimer of Opinion

When the auditor is unable to give any opinion in absence of necessary information, he is said to make a no opinion report or disclaimer of opinion.

Few situations leading to an adverse opinion are:

- Management preventing the auditor from observing all physical inventories and obtaining debtor's or creditor's confirmation or bank account balances
- Auditor may not have received the branch audit reports from the branch auditors
- There may be difference in trial balance
- Books of accounts destroyed in the fire of premises

The audit report may state that "The books of accounts were destroyed by the fire in the premises of the concern and were not available for examination. In the absence of books of accounts, we are unable to express any opinion on the accounts......."

iv)**Piecemeal or Partial Audit Report**

An auditor may decide to express his opinion about some of the items contained in the financial statements specially when he is not in a position to express his opinion about the entire financial statements of the entity due to absence of information.

The auditor may not be able to give an opinion on whether the accounts of the entire concern are true and fair but he may be able to give an opinion that the branch accounts are true and fair on the basis of branch audit report.

10.6 Companies (Auditor's Report) Order 2015 (Caro)

The Ministry of Corporate Affairs, Government of India notified Caro on 10th April 2015.

It shall apply to every company including foreign company except

i)A banking Company as defined in Clause (c0 of Section 5 of the Banking Regulation Act 1949

ii)An insurance company as defined under the Insurance Act 1938

iii)A company licensed to operate under section 8 of the Companies Act

iv)A small company as defined in Section 2 of the Companies Act

v)A One Person Company as defined under Section 2 of the Companies Act

vi) A private limited company with a paid up capital and reserves not more than Rs50 lakhs and which does not have loan outstanding exceeding 25 lakhs from any bank or financial institution and does not have a turnover exceeding Rs 5 crores at any point of time during the financial year.

10.6.1 Matters to be included in Auditor's Report

A. Fixed Assets

i) Whether the company has maintained proper records showing full quantitative details and situation of fixed assets.

ii) Whether these fixed assets have been physically verified by the management at reasonable intervals and material discrepancies if found, have been dealt with in the books of accounts

B. Internal Controls

The company has an adequate internal control system commensurate with the size of the company and the nature of the business for the purchase of inventory and fixed assets and for the sale of goods and services. The company is taking efforts to correct major weaknesses in internal control system.

C. Loans

Whether the company has granted any secured or unsecured loans to companies, firms and other parties and whether the receipt of principal and interest are regular. In case overdue amount is more than Rs 1 lakh rupees, whether the company takes reasonable steps to recover the principal and interest amount.

D. Inventory

- Whether the physical verification of inventory has been conducted by the management at regular intervals and whether the procedures of physical verification of inventory followed by the management are reasonable and adequate in relation to the size.
- Whether the company is maintaining proper records of inventory and material discrepancies if any have been properly dealt with in the books of accounts.

E. Orders passed by Courts or Tribunals

i)   Is the company regular in depositing undisputed statutory dues like the provident fund, employees state insurance, income tax and now GST etc with appropriate authorities and if not then the extent of the arears outstanding as at the last day of the financial year concerned from a period of six months from the date they are payable?

ii) In case the dues have not been deposited on account of any dispute, then the amount involved and the forum where dispute is pending shall be mentioned.

iii) Whether the amount required to be transferred to investor education and protection fund in accordance with the relevant provisions of the Companies Act 1956 and rules made thereunder has been transferred to such fund within time.

F. Maintenance of Cost Records

Where maintenance of cost records have been specified by the Central Government under sub-section1 of Section 148 of the New Act, where such accounts have been maintained

G. Accumulated Losses

Whether in case of a company which has been registered for a period of less than 5 years, its accumulated losses at the end of the financial year are not less than 50% of its net worth if the losses have been incurred in such financial years and the financial year immediately preceding such financial year also.

H. Acceptance of Deposits from Public

In case the company has accepted deposits and the relevant provisions have not been complied with and also the nature of contravention has to be stated.

I. Default in repayment of dues to bank or financial institution

Whether the company has defaulted in repayment of dues to the financial institution or bank or debenture holders and if yes, then the period of default to be reported.

J. Term loans

Whether term loans were applied for the purpose for which loans were obtained

K. Guarantee of loans taken by others

Whether the company has given any guarantee for loans taken by others from banks or any financial institutions, the terms and conditions which are prejudicial to the interest of the company

L. Reporting of Fraud

In case of any fraud on or by the company has been noticed, then the nature and amount so involved.

10.7 Changes in the Audit Report w.e.f April1,2018

A new format of Auditor's Report under SA 700 is effective for audit of Financial Statements for period beginning on or after April1, 2018.

The Standard on Auditing (SA) 700 deals with the auditor's responsibility to form an opinion on the financial statements. It also deals with the form and content of the auditor's report issued as a result of an audit of financial statements.

ICAI has released Illustrative Independent Auditor's Reports on Financial Statements in the following cases:

Illustration 1: An auditor's report on financial statements of a listed entity prepared in accordance with a fair presentation framework.

Illustration 2: An auditor's report on consolidated financial statements of a listed company prepared in accordance with a fair presentation framework

Illustration 3: Auditor's Report on Financial Statements of an Unlisted Company Prepared in Accordance with a Fair Presentation Framework

Illustration 4: Auditor's Report on Financial Statements of a Non Corporate Entity Prepared in accordance with a Fair Presentation

Illustration 5: Auditor's Report on Financial Statements of Non Corporate Entity in Accordance with a General Purpose Compliance Framework.

Below is the illustrative Auditor's Report on Financial Statements of an Unlisted Company Prepared in accordance with a Fair Presentation Framework.

Contents of Audit Report (As per Companies Act and Standards on Auditing)

Auditor's Report on the Standalone Financial Statements

Opinion

We have audited the accompanying Standalone Financial Statements of M/s ABC Private Limited (" the Company") which comprises the Balance Sheet as at March 31, 2018, the Statement of Profit and Loss (statement of changes in equity) and statement of cash flows for the year then ended, and notes to the financial statements including a summary of significant accounting policies and other explanatory information [in which are the Returns for the year ended on that date audited by the branch auditors of the Company's branches located at (location of branches)]

In our opinion and to the best of the information given to us, the aforesaid financial statements give the information required by the Act in the manner so required and give a true and fair view in conformity with the accounting principles generally accepted in India, of the state of affairs of the Company as at March 31, 20XX and profit/loss (changes in equity) and its cash flow for the year ended on that date.

Basis for Opinion

We conducted our audit in accordance with the Standards on Auditing (SAs) specified under section 143(10) of the Companies Act, 2013. Our responsibilities under those Standards are further described in the Auditor's Responsibilities for the Audit of the Financial Statements section of our report. We are independent of the Company in accordance with the Code of Ethics issued by the Institute of Chartered Accountants of India together with the ethical requirements that are relevant to our audit of the Financial Statements under the provisions of the Companies Act 2013 and the Rules thereunder and we have fulfilled our ethical responsibilities in accordance with these requirements and the Code of ethics. We believe that the audit evidence we have obtained is sufficient and appropriate to provide a basis for our opinion.

Responsibility of management for the Standalone Financial Statements

The Company's Board of Directors is responsible for the matters stated in section 134(5) of the Companies Act, 2013 with respect to the preparation of these standalone financial statements that give a true and fair view of the financial position, financial performance and cash flows of eth Company in accordance with the accounting principles generally accepted in India including the accounting Standards specified under section 133 of the Act. This responsibility also includes maintenance of adequate accounting records in accordance with the provisions of the

Act for safeguarding the assets of the Company and for preventing and detecting frauds and other irregularities; selection and application of appropriate implementation and maintenance of accounting policies; making judgement and estimates that are reasonable and prudent; and design, implementation and maintenance of adequate internal financial controls, that were operating effectively for ensuring the accuracy and completeness of the accounting records, relevant to the preparation and presentation of the financial statement that give a true and fair view and are free from material misstatement, whether due to fraud or error.

In preparing the financial statements, management is responsible for assessing the Company's ability to continue as a going concern, disclosing as applicable, matters related to going concern and using the going concern basis of accounting unless management either intends to liquidate the Company or to cease operations, or has no realistic alternative but to do so.

Those Board of Directors are also responsible for overseeing the company's financial reporting process.

Auditor's Responsibility for the Audit of the Financial Statements

Our objectives are to obtain reasonable assurance about whether the financial statements as a whole are free from material misstatement, whether due to fraud or error, and to issue an auditor's report that includes our opinion. Reasonable assurance is a high level of assurance but is not a guarantee that an audit conducted in accordance with SAs will always detect a material misstatement when it exists. Misstatements can arise from fraud or error and are considered material if, individually or in the aggregate, they could be reasonably be expected to influence the economic decisions of users taken on the basis of these financial statements.

Other Matter

We did not audit the financial statements/ information of ....(number) branches included in the standalone financial statements of the company whose financial statements/ financial information reflect total assets of Rs ....as at 31st March 20XX and total revenue of Rs .... for the year ended on that date, as considered in the standalone financial statements/ information of these branches have been audited by the branch auditors whose reports have been furnished to us, and our opinion in so far as it relates to the amounts and disclosures included in respect of branches, is based solely on the reports of such branch auditors.

Report on Other Legal and Regulatory Requirements

As required by the Companies (Auditor's Report) Order, 2016 issued by the Central Government of India in terms of sub-section (11) of Section 143 of the Companies Act, 2013, we give in the Annexure a statement on the matters specified in paragraphs 3 and 4 of the Order, to the extent applicable.

As required by Section 143(3) of the Act, we report that:

We have sought and obtained all the information and explanations which to the best of our knowledge and belief were necessary for the purposes of our audit.

a.In our opinion, proper books of account as required by law have been kept by the Company so far as it appears from our examination of those books [and proper returns adequate for the purposes of our audit have been received from the branches not visited by us.

b.[The reports on the accounts of the branch offices of the Company audited under Section 143(8) of the Act by branch auditors have been sent to us and have been properly dealt with by us in preparing this report.

c.The Balance Sheet, the Statement of Profit and Loss, and the Cash Flow Statement dealt with by this Report are in agreement with the books of accounts [and with the returns received from the branches not visited by us]

d.In our opinion the aforesaid standalone financial statements comply with the Accounting Standards specified under Section 133 of the Act, read with Rule 7 of the Companies (Accounts) Rules, 2014.

e.On the basis of the written representations received from the directors as on 31st March, 20XX taken on record by the Board of Directors, none of the directors is disqualified as on

31st March, 20XX from being appointed as a director in terms of Section 164(2) of the Act.

e.With respect to the adequacy of the internal financial controls over financial reporting of the Company and the operating effectiveness of such controls, refer to our separate Report in "Annexure A'.

g. With respect to the other matters to be included in the auditor's Report in accordance with Rule 11 of the Companies (Audit and Auditor's) Rule 2014, in our opinion and to the best of our information and according to the explanations given to us:

i)The Company has disclosed the impact of pending litigations on its financial position in its financial statements-Refer Note XX to the financial statements; [or the Company does not have any pending litigations which would impact its financial statements.

ii)The Company has made provision, as required under the applicable law or accounting standards, for material foreseeable losses. If any, on long-term contracts including derivative contracts-Refer Note XX to the financial statements; [or the Company did not have any long-term contracts including derivative contracts for which there were any material foreseeable losses.

iii)There has been no delay in transferring amounts, required to be transferred to the Investor Education and Protection Fund by the Company [or, following are the instances of delay in transferring to the Investor and Protection Fund by the Company or there were no amounts which were required to be transferred to the Investor Education and Protection Fund by the Company.

For ABC & Co
Chartered Accountants
Firm Regn. No.........

(..................)
Partner

Place

....
Membership   No.......

Date............

10.8 True and Fair Concept

The term 'True and correct' of the Companies Act 1913 was subsequently replaced by the term 'True and fair' of the Companies Act 1956. 'True and fair view' in auditing means that the financial statements are free from material misstatements and also represent the financial performance of the company faithfully. The term 'true' means that the financial statements are factually correct and has been prepared by the applicable reporting framework and do not contain any material misstatements that may mislead the users. 'Fair' means that the financial statements present the information without any bias and reflect the economic substance of transactions.

The guiding factors of 'true and fair view are:

- Material information has been properly disclosed
- Generally accepted accounting principles have been properly disclosed
- Financial statements have been prepared as per regulatory requirements
- Disclosure of exceptional and non-recurring items have been properly made
- Proper care has been taken of events occurring after balance sheet date and prior to the submission of audit report
- There is no window dressing or secret reserve as well as no understatement or overstatement.

10.9 Materiality

The concept of 'materiality' means that trivial matters are to be disregarded and essential matters to be disclosed. As per SA-320 (revised) 'Materiality on planning and performing an audit" misstatements including omissions are considered to be material, if they individually or in aggregate, could reasonably be expected to influence the economic decisions of the users taken on the basis of the financial statements.

The auditor's determination is a matter of professional judgement. Materiality is a relative term. What may be material in one circumstance may be immaterial in another.

The guiding factors to determine materiality are:

i)The nature of transaction is an important factor. For example, a transaction of small amount may be material if occurring unusually but may be immaterial if occurring routinely.

ii)The size or amount involved is another factor. For example, Rs 2000 may be material for a small concern but not a big one.

iii)An item may be immaterial separately but material in aggregate.

iv)Relative significance may be another factor. For example, If an item belongs to a group, it should be considered in a group and not separately like current assets should be considered in relation to total asset

v)The materiality may be considered by comparing it with the corresponding figures of the previous years.

vi) In prior periods, misstatements have been considered immaterial and may have been ignored accordingly. Such misstatements may affect the financial information of the current period.

vii)Deviation from regulatory requirement is considered as material even if the deviation is minor.

10.10 SA 710 Comparative Information – Corresponding Figures and Comparative Financial Statements

SA 710 deals with the responsibilities of an auditor with respect to comparative information in the audit of the financial statements.

When the audit of prior period financial statements has been executed by a predecessor auditor or the financial statements weren't audited, the guidance and opening balances are also applicable.

i)Nature of comparative Information

The nature of the comparative information which is presented in financial statements of the entity is governed by the requirements of relevant reporting framework.

The two approaches to the reporting responsibilities of an auditor in respect of comparative information include:

a)**Corresponding figures** - In case of corresponding figures, only the current period is referred for the opinion of the auditor on financial services.

b)**Comparative financial statements** – In case of comparative financial statements, each period for which such financial statements are presented is referred for the purpose of auditor's opinion.

ii)Objectives

The objectives of the auditor are:

- To obtain sufficient appropriate audit evidence about whether the comparative information included in the financial statements has been presented in all material respects in accordance with the applicable financial reporting framework.
- To report in accordance with the auditor's reporting responsibilities.

iii) Audit Procedures

An auditor should consider whether financial statements comprises comparative information which are required by relevant financial reporting framework and whether the information so required are classified appropriately.

An auditor to achieve this purpose should assess whether:

- The comparative information is in agreement with amounts and other disclosures provided in the prior period
- The accounting policies shown in comparative information are consistent with the ones applied currently. In case of changes in accounting policies, whether same are accounted, presented and disclosed adequately and appropriately

iv) Audit Reporting

a) Corresponding Figures

In case of presentation of corresponding figures, the opinion of an auditor shouldn't refer to corresponding figures barring the following situations:

1. If auditor's report on the financial statement of the prior period include a disclaimer of opinion, a qualified opinion or an adverse opinion and matters that required modification are unresolved.

2. If an auditor gathers audit evidence that the material misstatement exists in financial statements of the prior period in which previously an unmodified opinion was issued.

3.In case financial statements of the prior period weren't audited.

In case of the circumstances mentioned in the first situation, the auditor   should modify his audit opinion on financial statements of the current period. The auditor should either do the following:

The auditor should refer to the corresponding figures in the description of the matter requiring modification when effects or likely effects of such matter on the figures of the current period are material.

Or

The auditor in other cases should explain that his audit opinion has been modified due to the effects or likely effects of an unresolved matter on comparability of figures of the existing period and such corresponding figures.

Two cases for the same are as follows:

---

1. Prior period Financial Statements audited by a Predecessor Auditor

In case the audit of prior period financial statements was performed by a predecessor auditor and the law permits auditor to refer to the report of the predecessor auditing on corresponding figures, the auditor should state in the Other Matter paragraph in his audit report

a)That the audit of prior period financial statements was performed by a predecessor auditor

---

b) Type of opinion which was expressed by such predecessor auditor and the reason if the opinion is modified

c)The date of such report

---

2. Prior period Financial statements not audited

In case of the unaudited financial statements of the prior period, the auditor should state the same in another matter paragraph in his audit report that such corresponding figures are unaudited.

However, such a statement doesn't relieve an auditor from his duty of obtaining sufficient audit evidence that opening balances are free of material misstatements which affect the financial statements of the current period.

B. Comparative Financial Statement

In case of presentation of comparative financial statements, each period for which such financial statements are presented and audit opinion is expressed should be referred for auditor's opinion.

In case of the opinion of the auditor on the financial statements of prior period differs from the opinion expressed by the auditor previously, the auditor should disclose applicable reasons for such different opinion in the Other Matter paragraph as per SA 7068

Two cases for the same are as follows:

1. Prior period Financial Statements audited by a Predecessor Auditor

In case the audit of prior period financial statements was performed by a predecessor auditor, the auditor should in addition to expressing the opinion on financial statements of the current period, state in the Other Matter paragraph in his audit report

a)That the audit of prior period financial statements was performed by a predecessor auditor

b) Type of opinion which was expressed by such predecessor auditor and the reason if the opinion is modified

c)The date of such report

2. Prior period Financial statements not audited

In case of the unaudited financial statements of the prior period, the auditor should state the same in another matter paragraph in his audit report that such corresponding figures are unaudited.

However, such a statement doesn't relieve an auditor from his duty of obtaining sufficient audit evidence that opening balances are free of material misstatements which affect the financial statements of the current period.

10.11 SA -720 Auditor's Responsibility in relation to Other Information

SA 720 defines other information as financial or non-financial information (other than financial statements and the auditor's report thereon) included in an entity's annual report.

Annual reports include a lot of quantitative information. The information provided to annual reports is used by users of the financial statements to analyse the risk associated with business and in decision making.

Following are considered as annual reports:

- Management report, operating and financial review or similar reports charged by governance as director's report
- Chairman's statement
- Corporate governance reports

Following are not other information within the scope of the SA

- Corporate Social Responsibility Report
- Sustainability Report
- Diversity reports
- Human rights reports
- Labour practices reports
- Separate industry reports prepared in the banking, insurance and pension industries
- Other regulatory filings with eth government agencies such as the Registrar of Companies

The revised standard on auditing is effective for audits of financial statements for periods beginning on or after 1 April 2018.

10.11.1 Objectives and scope of SA 720 (Revised)

SA 720 (Revised) increases the responsibility of the auditor relating to other information in enhancing the reliability of financial statements. The auditor's responsibilities apply regardless of whether the other information is obtained by the auditor prior to or after the date of the auditor's report.

The scope of SA720 (revised) is written in the context of an audit of financial statements by an independent auditor. The auditor's opinion on the financial statements does not cover the other information nor does this SA require to obtain audit evidence beyond that required to form an opinion on the financial statements.

The SA 720 (Revised) requires an auditor to read and consider the other information where:

- There is material inconsistency between the other information and the financial statements
- There is material inconsistency between the other information and the auditor's knowledge obtained in the audit.

Such material misstatements may undermine the creditability of the financial statements and also inappropriately influence the economic decisions of the users for whom the auditor's report is prepared.

10.11.2 Auditor's role in respect to other information

The auditor should make appropriate arrangements with the management of a company to obtain other information in a timely manner and if possible prior to the auditor's report.

The auditor should remain alert for indicators that the other information not related to the financial statements appears to be materially misstated. The auditor should include in his audit documentation the procedures performed and final version of the other information on which auditor has performed his procedures.

When the other information is obtained after the date of the auditor's report, the auditor is not required to update the procedures performed in accordance with the requirement of SA560, subsequent Event. However, the auditor would communicate with management or those charged with governance about the possible implications when the other information is obtained after the date of the auditor's report.

10.11.3 Reporting by auditors under SA720 (revised)

The auditor's report would include a separate section with a heading 'Other Information' or other appropriate heading at the date of the auditor's report.

- The auditor has obtained or expects to obtain the other information for an audit of financial statements of a listed entity.
- The auditor has obtained some or all of the other information for an audit of financial statements of an unlisted corporate entity.

The auditor's report will include:

- A statement that management is responsible for other information
- Identification of the other information obtained prior to the date of the auditor's report. In the case of the listed company, the auditor is also required to identify any other information expected to be obtained after the date of the auditor's report
- A statement that the auditor's opinion does not cover the other information and accordingly, the auditor does not express an audit opinion or any form of assurance conclusion thereon.
- A description of the auditor's responsibilities relating to reading, considering and reporting on other information
- When other information has been obtained prior to the date of the auditor's report either

    i)A statement that the auditor has nothing to report or

    ii)In case the auditor has concluded if there is an incorrect material misstatement, a statement that describes the incorrected material misstatements of the other information

Conclusion

- The revision of SA 720 aims to clarify and increase the auditor's involvement with other information – whether financial or non-financial information other than audited financial statements that is included in the entity's annual report.
- The auditors are not required to obtain assurance about the other information

- The auditor's report will include a separate section on other information when the auditor has obtained some or all of the other information as of the date of the audit report.
- In case of listed entities, 'Other information' section includes if the auditor expects to obtain other information after the date of the auditor's report.

10.12 Auditor's Certificate

An auditor's certificate is a written confirmation of the accuracy of the facts stated therein and does not involve any estimate or opinion. The concern needs a certificate from the auditor for the following

- Import or export licence
- Certificate of bonus shares
- Certificate for issue of other shares
- Certificate of computation of bonus
- Certificate for public deposits
- Certificate on consumption of raw material

10.12.1 Auditor's duty

i)The primary responsibility for the contents of the certificates is of the management. Auditor should make it clear in his certificate that he has checked the particulars and submitted by the concern.

ii)Auditor should clearly understand the scope, nature and terms of his work. He should obtain the details of scope etc in writing from the management to avoid understanding.

iii)The auditor should obtain advice of an expert and make clear that he has relied on such advice in case required for purely technical advice.

iv)The form of the certificate may be prescribed by law or may be designed by the auditor himself.

iv)A certificate should have following contents:

- Identify the items certified
- State how the items were checked and verified
- State any limitations in scope
- State the assumptions made in the certificate
- To specify if the certificate is based on the audited accounts and the name of the auditor
- Certificate should be comprehensive and self-contained. It should not give reference to any other report attached to it.
- Certificate can be addressed to the client or to the public authority

10.12.2 Comparison between Audit certificate and Audit report

The difference between audit report and audit certificate are:

Points of differences	Audit Report	Audit Certificate
Concept	It is an opinion on the final accounts of the concern	It is written confirmation of facts

Scope	It covers entire books of accounts	It covers only specific items e.g. bonus computation
Form	Form is standard as prescribed by law	No standard format
Period	It pertains to one year	Certificate may cover more or less than one accounting year
Responsibility	Auditor is responsible for giving opinion after due care	Certified auditor is responsible for accuracy of facts certified
Qualified report	Auditor can give a qualified report	Qualified certificate is not possible
Users	Audit report is used by owners, shareholders, management , banks etc	Certificates are used by bank or the specific users

Chapter 11

Auditing in Computerised Environment

Introduction

SA 401/Auditing and Assurance Standard 29(AAS-29), issued by ICAI in April 2013, deals with auditing in a Computer System Environment (EDP audit). It aims to establish standards on procedures to be followed when an audit is conducted in a Computer Information System Environment (CISE).

Nowadays, the corporate world is getting more and more inclined towards the use of information technology in their day to day work. This has changed the way the organisations carry out their operations and various business processes. Auditing in CISE has not changed the fundamental nature of auditing though but has brought substantial changes in the method of evidence collection and evaluation. CISE exists when a computer is involved in the processing of financial information relevant to the audit. There may be one or more computers of different sizes involved in the entity. The auditor needs to have knowledge about computer environment (hardware, software etc) and keep pace with rapidly changing technology.

11.1 Difference between auditing of manual accounts and Computerised accounts and Problems in shifting from manual to computer accounting

S.No	Manual Accounts auditing system	Computerised accounts auditing system
1.	It is simple and therefore, can be understood by the auditor quickly	It is complex and therefore requires technical expertise and knowledge by the auditor
2	Audit trail includes trial balance and other records and source document, journal entries, ledger	Audit trail consists of magnetic tapes, punch cards, discs, printouts. There is lack of audit trail in this system.
3.	Based on segregation of duties	Based on segregation of knowledge
4.	Scheduling of audit planning is not very tight	Involves tighter scheduling of audit planning as the auditor has to make arrangements to provide auditor access to computer system and various files
5.	Errors are not repeated in nature	Errors in a computer system are of serious matter as an erroneous programme will always execute data incorrectly
6.	Errors can be corrected by feedback given by the auditor	Extensive redesigning and reprogramming is requited to rectify them

The problems faced by shifting from the manual based accounting to computer based accounting are:

i)Visual observation is difficult because of the speed of the computer. The slowing down of the system may be of no value to the auditor as it is difficult to understand the electronic pulses.

ii)There can be changes in the program those can be done without auditor's knowledge.

iii)Audit trail may be explained as those documents, records, journals, ledgers and master files those enable an auditor to trace the transactions from the source to the summarised totals in the accounting period.

iv)High level computer languages may not be understood by the auditor.

11.2 Factors to be considered by auditor while auditing in computerised environment

An auditor needs to keep following factors in mind while auditing in computerised environment:

- The overall scope and aim of audit does not alter in a CISE.
- The use of computer changes the processing, storage, retrieval and communication of financial information. CISE affects the procedures for study of internal control, evaluation of the audit risks and tests of control and substantive procedures.
- The auditor should consider the extent of use of CISE to process accounting information, system of internal control in use and effect of CISE on audit trail.

- An auditor should have sufficient knowledge of CISE to plan , direct, supervise, review the work done.
- He should be able to understand the infrastructure of the CIS, significance of accounting application, availability of data, availability of reports, availability of Computer Assisted Audit Technique and knowledge of EDP vocabulary and terminology.
- Auditor should evaluate the controls in CISE by studying whether the system ensures:
  - i) Complete and correct inputs, processing and input
  - ii) Provides for timely detection of errors and frauds
  - iii) Provides data security against power/hardware failures
  - iv) Prevents unauthorised changes to programs, data, reports etc

11.3 Nature of audit risks in CISE

The risk in audit in CISE may be general or specific.

i)General risks relate to general CIS activities such as program development and maintenance, system software support etc

ii)Specific risks relate to errors and frauds in specific applications, in specific data.

An auditor should understand the nature of risks of the CISE :

i)A programmer may act as a data entry operator leading to weak internal control ii)An error in software or hardware will result in errors in all transactions due to uniform processing

iii)Few transactions may be started automatically without authorisation.

iv)Scope of error in CISE is more due to unauthorised access or manipulation of data

An auditor in order to reduce audit risks to a low level should design audit procedures in consideration of CISE. He should document the audit plan, the nature and timing of audit procedures performed and the audit conclusions thereon.

11.4 Approaches to auditing in computerized environment

There are two types of audit procedures:

i)Black box approach i.e. auditing around computer

ii)White box approach i.e. auditing through computers

11.4.1 Auditing around the computer

Auditing around the computer involves arriving at the audit conclusion through examining the internal control system for a computer installation and the input and output of the application systems. The auditor thereon infers the quality of the processing control. Application control processing is not examined directly but the auditor views the computer as a black box i.e. concentrates on input and output and ignores the data processing. He assumes, processing would be accurate if inputs and outputs are correct.

The auditor usually audits around the computer when the system is simple and batch oriented and the system uses generalised software that is well-tested and used wisely.

Advantages

The basic advantages of auditing around the computer

- It is simple
- Audit cost is low
- Auditor with limited technical knowledge of computers can be trained easily to perform the audit.

Disadvantages

The basic demerits of auditing around the computer

- It cannot be used for systems having complexity in terms of size.
- Time consuming and expensive as lot of printing of data is required
- The auditor may not be able to assess the likelihood of the system depending upon the environmental changes.

11.4.2 Auditing through Computers

When the use of computer is made by the auditor to carry out compliance and substantive procedures, it is called auditing through the computer. He focusses upon all phases of CIS activities i.e. input, processing and output.

The auditor reviews and tests general and application controls and determine their effectiveness and then determines the nature, timing and extent of substantive procedures. The auditor uses audit techniques of enquiry, observation and documentation to gather about the general controls. The auditor may use computer-aided test techniques to test application controls in this procedure.

The process of auditing is not simple but involves exposure, experience and application of knowledge and expertise to different circumstances. It is required that the auditor need not only have adequacy of knowledge regarding information requirement but also may be exposed to system.

The need for using auditing through computers are:

i)The application system produces large volume of input and output that makes direct examination of the validity of input and output difficult.

ii)The logic of the system is complex that there are large portions those facilitate use of the system or efficient processing

iii)There are substantial gaps in the visible audit due to cost-benefit considerations

iv)Important parts of the internal control systems are there in the computer system.

v)To make processing and analysis more efficient.

Benefits

The benefit of auditing through computers is:

- Reduces cost as print-outs are not required
- The auditor has increased power to effectively test a computer system.
- The confidence of the auditor regarding data processing increases.

- The auditor is able to assess the system's ability to cope with environment change.

Demerits

The demerit of auditing through computers are

- High costs involved
- The need for extensive technical expertise when systems are complex.

However, the merits outweigh the demerits and hence auditing through computer is the only viable method of carrying out the audit.

11.5 Effects of Computers on Auditing

The objective and scope of auditing do not undergo a big change in a CIS environment. Auditor must provide a competent, independent opinion as to whether the financial statements report a true and fair view of the state of affairs of an entity. However, computer systems have affected how auditors collects and evaluates evidence.

A. Changes to Evidence Collection

Auditors need to face a series of diverse and complex range of internal control technology that did not exist in manual system

i)Accurate operations of a disk drive may require a set of hardware controls not required in the manual system

ii)System development control includes procedures for testing programs that are not necessary in manual control

The auditors need to face these challenges in evidence collection:

i)Understanding the rapid changes in hardware and software technology is not easy

ii)In case the auditor is not able to keep up with these developments, it will become difficult to evaluate the reliability of communication network competently.

iii)The continuous development of control technology also makes it more difficult for auditors to collect evidence on the reliability of controls.

iv)Auditors have to run through computer systems themselves if they have to collect the necessary evidences sometimes.

B. Changes in evidence evaluation

Auditors need to understand:

i) whether a control is functioning reliably
ii) Traceability of control strength and weakness through the system

The auditors have to face the following challenges in evaluation of evidences in a CIS environment:

i)Consequences of errors in a computer system are serious matters as errors in a computer system may be deterministic i.e. an erroneous program will always execute data incorrectly

ii) As the errors are generated at high speed and the cost and effort to correct and rerun program may be high iii)Errors in computer program may involve extensive redesign and reprogramming. So, high quality computer system may be designed, implemented and operated upon.

iv)The auditor needs to ensure that controls are sufficient to maintain assets safeguarding, data integrity and system effectiveness.

11.6 Computer Aided Audit Techniques (CAAT)

Computer Aided Techniques or CAATs are such techniques applied through the computer which are used in verifying the data being processed. They are computer programs and data that the auditor uses as part of the audit procedures to process data of audit significance contained in an entity's information system. CAATs is the audit tool those auditor uses for enhancing the effectiveness and efficiency of audit procedures.

The demand for the use of the computer aided audit techniques arises from:

- There is absence of input document and the data may be entered directly into the computer system without supporting documents.
- Certain data may be maintained on computer files only. The lack of visible audit trail may necessitate the use of computer aided technique and it may exist for a limited period of time.
- The lack of visible output may result in the need to access data retained on machine readable files.
- There may be access to data or programs by unauthorised persons inside or outside the entity.

A. Benefits of CAATs

The merits of CAAT are the following:

- The effectiveness and efficiency of audit procedures may improve through the use of CAAT in obtaining and evaluating audit evidence.
- The auditor may save his time by evaluating the EDP controls using CAAT than through other audit procedures.
- CAAT allows effective examination-in-depth of selected transactions since the auditor constructs the lost audit trail.
- CAAT may be used for performing audit procedures such as test of details of transactions and balances, analytical procedures, sampling programs and re-performing calculations performed by the entity's accounting system

B. Few techniques of CAAT

i)Test Data Approach

In this technique, the auditor prepares transaction data (test data) and processes it on the client's processing system under his control. If results of processing match with the pre-determined output, this shows that the applications and general controls are functioning well. Further, test data's should test each control on which he wishes to rely.

The merits of this technique are

- It is reliable,

- Easy to use
- Economical in the long run.

The disadvantages are:

- It puts additional work on the auditor
- High additional cost
- Difficulties in designing test data

ii)Integrated Test Data Approach

In this technique, the auditor creates fictitious within the client's actual data. The historical data are thus integrated with actual client data and processed. Subsequently, it is removed by reversing journal entries or through programme commands and then financial reports are complied.

The merits of this technique are:

- Gives assurance that the program being tested by the auditor have actually been used by the client
- Long term economies

The disadvantages are:

- High Initial costs
- Difficult to ensure whether fictitious transactions do not impact actual results
- Errors may be detected but well laid frauds may be difficult to detect

iii)Generalised Audit Software (GAS)

Audit programs are designed by computer manufacturers, software professionals and large firms of auditors in this technique.

GAS helps in performing following functions:

- Examination and review of records based on auditor's criteria
- Selection and printing of audit samples
- Testing calculations and performing comparisons
- Comparing data on separate files
- Summarising data and performing analysis
- Comparing actual data with client's records

The benefits of GAS are:

- It will assist auditor to carry out compliance and substantive procedures
- It helps to examine each transaction
- It is a reliable technique

The disadvantages of this technique are:

The technique is dependent on the availability of client's data, auditor's ingenuity and strength of client's internal control system

11.7 Auditing in SAP environment

Enterprise Resource Planning (ERP) systems integrate the majority of company's business processes by sharing common data and practices across the organisation. Since the 1990s, businesses have been managing their operations with ERPs which have enabled centralized control over operations by implementing a common data model and integrated business processes. SAP has been a pioneer from the start and uses a process-driven approach to match business processes with application processes.

Many business organizations uses SAP application to help them plan their resources and activities. Its range and flexibility makes it a challenge to audit. SAP is highly configurable and implementations often vary, even within various business units of a company-both financial and non-financial. It is extremely important to gain a good understanding of how SAP is being used in the business while planning the audit approach and scope.

Auditing a SAP environment introduces several unique complexities that can affect the scope. The ERP audit involves a comprehensive review of the existing ERP system in terms of its functional performance. Initially, a full-fledged mapping of the existing business process in relation to the application software is carried out. It is on this basis that the utilization of all functional modules is evaluated.

i) Business processes

SAP covers most business processes and a minor change in the business process can have a direct impact on the audit procedures to be performed. Changes in the setup and configuration of the system, the release strategy of creating new processes may result in new module of SAP and thus involve more audit risks.

To illustrate, a client may consider retiring its old purchasing system and moving onto SAP. Earlier, major controls over purchase order approval may have been performed manually. However, with the SAP implementation, the client wants to automate the approval process in SAP. Therefore, adequate controls are maintained to reduce the risks and would involve testing automated controls instead of the manual controls over purchase order.

ii)Segregation of duty

The auditor needs to understand the design of SAP authorisation concept for an effective audit. Poor security design results in users being given access to unauthorised transactions. Hence the review of the design and implementation of SAP security and access controls is needed to ensure segregation of duties and thus the access to sensitive transactions is well controlled.

Segregation of duty conflicts can arise when a user is given access to two or more conflicting transactions like creating a sales order and amending vendor master details. A clear mapping of the business processes and identification of roles and responsibilities is involved in the process.

Apart from that, there may be transactions or access levels that are considered sensitive to the business such as reviewing G/L codes and structures, amending recurring entries and deleting audit logs. Such sensitive transactions need to be considered during the planning phase.

iii)Types of Controls

There are four types of controls in SAP that an audit client can utilise so as to create a secure environment: inherent controls, configuration controls, application security and manual reports of SAP reports.

Configurable controls are executed by SAP system and are preventive in nature. However, manual controls including manual review of reports are executed by an employee and are mainly defective in nature. For example, there are standard automated controls such as three-way matching i.e. matching of purchase orders, good receipt and invoices. The client may opt for four-way matching or two-way matching, thus requiring compensation to suit specific processes.

Owing to the complexity of SAP application, each client uses a different mix of controls so as to achieve their specific control objectives. Hence, the audit approach needs to be tailored for each situation appropriately.

In SAP, it is essential to understand the link between configurable controls and access controls. There may be a mix of configurable and access controls that create a control solution. To illustrate, 'Purchase Orders over Rs 10 lacs must be approved by the manager.' This looks like an access control but is a configurable control as well due to configuration needed for the release strategy. In fact, these are complimentary controls, two controls covering the same risk together.

iv) Process risks

SAP is a process based ERP system and each SAP may have different risks associated with it. Each client has different business processes, products and services and systems that suit the environment. It is important to design the process effectively in SAP to reduce the risks associated with inadequate or failed business processes. Thus, an effective audit approach should include an evaluation of risks and an understanding of the mapping of business process for each SAP instance.

v)Rotation Plan

SAP is highly customisable, process driven and enables a range of control selections and thus would have a different risk profile. Also, the risk profile of different modules and sub-modules such as financials (FI), materials management (MM), sales and distribution (SD), payroll, Business information warehouse(BW) will be different.

The vast areas of the business operations of SAP application make it impractical to cover them all in one single audit. It is appropriate to consider a rotation plan in order to complete a comprehensive audit of SAP. It involves planning reviews of business processes, module, sub-module, system configuration and change management including design of segregation of duties and access levels. It ensures that the audits are performed using appropriately skilled resources and cover each risk area. These areas should be assessed effectively to identify gaps in control weaknesses and recommend appropriate steps to resolve the issues.

vi)Risk-based approach

SAP systems are also upgraded and enhanced periodically to meet ever-changing business requirements. Companies are faced with changing risks in the environment that affect their business processes in the current economic climate.

The aim of risk-based approach is to allow the auditors to find the areas of high-risk potential and give greater focus to them while planning the audit. The risk-based approach should include general risk analysis, analytical audit procedures, systems and substantive testing. Thus, an auditor should conduct the audit efficiently with a degree of reliability along with optimising the time and effort. It is therefore advisable that a top-down risk-based audit approach is adopted to effectively review SAP.

Chapter 12

Auditing in the Decade Ahead: Challenge and Change regarding IAASB and PCAOB

Introduction

There is a lot happening in audit environment which is constantly changing. Nowadays, financial reporting continues to evolve more complex, more areas of judgement and more qualitative disclosures. As a result of the financial crisis, some key questions were raised about the quality of effectiveness and the role of professional skepticism and judgement and also the relevance of the audit.

As a result, there are many important ongoing debates on auditing now happening in Europe, North America and elsewhere. These debates acknowledge the importance of ongoing and structured dialogues among and between many stakeholders.

It is very clear throughout history that there has been a strong call for professional accountants to act in the public interest and to take into account the expectations society places on them and to understand these expectations and respond to them through meaningful interactions. Therefore, interactions are an essential and fundamental principal underpinning what we do.

With this backdrop, lets highlight some of the key responses to IAASB and PCAOB's key responses to current developments.

12.1 IAASB (The International Auditing and Assurance Standards Board)

IAASB is an independent standards body which issues standards like the International Standards on Auditing, quality control guidelines and other services, to support the international auditing of financial statements. It is a body supported by the International Federation of Accountants (IFAC). Founded in March 1978 as the international Auditing Practices Committee (IAPC), the IAASB's current strategic themes include:

- Enhancing the role, relevancy and quality of assurance in an audit
- Supporting global financial stability
- Facilitating implementation of the standards it sets

IAASB currently intends to finalize a new publication entitled **'A Framework for Audit Quality: Key Elements that create an Environment for Audit Quality'.** The main goal for this Framework is to raise awareness of the key elements of audit quality, encourage key stakeholders to reflect on ways to improve audit quality and promote dialogue between stakeholders. The Framework is qualitative in nature, describing not only the environment for audit quality at the engagement firm and national levels but also their interrelationships. It works on input, process and output factors as well as interactions in the financial reporting supply chain and contextual factors.

Focus is laid on input and process factors such as standards, methodology, education and training etc. Output factors mean what users of financial statements see and read on which they base their perceptions and conclusions of audit quality. Auditors need to respond properly to context factors also such as culture, corporate governance and the regulatory regime and litigation environment which have impact on financial reporting directly or indirectly.

12.1.1 New Proposals for Audit Reporting

The IAASB unanimously approved and released a comprehensive exposure draft of proposed new and revised international Standards on Auditing (ISAs) addressing reporting on audited financial statements.

There are many important changes proposed to the auditor's report – for example, clarification of the responsibilities of the auditor and importance to the auditor's opinion. One of the more fundamental charges proposed is **NEW ISA 701, Communicating Key Audit matters in the Independent Auditor's Report.** Communicating key audit matters require professional judgment and a careful consideration of what is unique about the specific entity and the specific audit undertaken- and therefore the matters of relevance to audit report users and the entity's financial statements.

The new standard directs the auditor to select key audit matters from those communicated with the audit committee. There is a concern that this may prompt the auditor to not communicate certain matters to the audit committee if there is pressure from management against bringing further transparency to an issue. Henceforth, the standard should indicate a broader source from which the auditor would consider the matters to communicate in the auditor's report.

12.1.1.a Determination of KAM

There are three matters which the ISA requires to take into account when making the determination.

1.Areas which were considered to be susceptible to higher risks of material misstatement or which were deemed to be 'significant risks' in accordance with ISA 315 (Revised), *Identifying Assessing the Risks of material Misstatement through Understanding the Entity and its Environment.*

2. Significant auditor judgments in relation to areas of the financial statements that involved significant management judgment. It might include accounting estimates which have been identified by the auditor as having a high degree of estimation uncertainty.

3. The effect of the audit of significant events or transactions that have taken place during the period.

The matters those are more significant to the auditor in the audit of financial statements is regarded as KAM.

12.1.1.b Communicating KAM

The auditor must ensure that each matter is appropriately described in the audit report once the auditor has determined which matters will be included as KAM.

1.Why the matter was determined to be one of most significance and hence a key matter and

2. How the matter was described in the audit which may include a description of the auditor's approach, a brief overview of procedures performed with an indication of their outcome and any key observations in respect of the matter

12.1.1.c Reporting in line with ISA 570, *Going Concern*

The work of the auditor has been enhanced in ISA570 (Revised), *Going Concern* and the ISA includes additional guidance relating to the appropriateness of disclosures when a material uncertainty exists.

Under ISA 570 (Revised), the auditor will continue to express an unmodified opinion if the use of the going concern basis of accounting exists and management have included adequate disclosures relating to the material uncertainties. However, the auditor must include a separate section under the heading 'Material Uncertainty Related to Going Concern'

The section headed 'Material Uncertainty Related to Going Concern' is included immediately after the Basis for Opinion paragraph but before the KAM section. By their very nature, issues identified relating to going concern are likely to be considered a key audit matter and hence needs to be communicated in the auditor's report.

To summarise, if a confirmed material uncertainty exists, it must be disclosed in accordance with ISA 570 and where there is a 'close call' over going concern which has been determined by the auditor to be a KAM, it should be disclosed in line with ISA 701.

12.2 PCAOB (Public Company Accounting Oversight Board)

The Public Company Accounting Oversight Board (PCAOB) is a private-sector, non-profit corporation created by the Sarbanes – Oxley act of 2012 to oversee the audits of public companies and other issuers in order to protect the interests of investors and further the public interest in the preparation of informative, accurate and independent audit reports.

The PCAOB has four primary functions in overseeing these auditors: registration, inspection, standard setting and enforcement. Under Section 101 of the Sarbanes-Oxley Act, the PCAOB has the power to:

- register public accounting firms that prepare audit reports for issuers and broker-dealers;
- set auditing quality control, ethics, independence and other standards relating to audit reports of issuers;
- conduct inspections of PCAOB-registered public accounting firms;
- conduct investigations and disciplinary proceedings;
- perform such other duties or functions as the Board determines are necessary;
- sue and be sued, complain and defend in its corporate name and through its own counsel with the approval of the SEC;
- allocate, assess and collect accounting support fees that fund the Board;
- conduct its operations, maintain offices and exercise all its rights and powers in any part of the United States

- enter into contracts, execute instruments, incur liabilities

12.2.1 The PCAOB's policy agenda to enhance the relevance, credibility and transparency of audits

i. The Auditor's Reporting Model

The PCAOB released a concept release on the potential changes to the auditor's reporting model to respond to investor's call. There are many practical challenges as to who the client is, so that the auditor's report is more informative for investors. To illustrate, we need to think what the auditors are capable of or producing for general use within the short filling periods.

There needs to be consistency of reporting. Investors ought to be able to expect that differences in reports reflect differences in the quality of the financial reporting subject to audit.

The alternatives described in the PCAOB's concept release aim at enhancing the relevance of the auditor's communication to investors. This would not change the fundamental role of the auditor to perform an audit and attest to management assertions as in the management's financial statements. It does not intend to put the auditor in the position of reporting financial information for management.

ii.   Auditor Independence

The PCAOB is focussed on auditor independence and issued a concept release to seek public comment on how to enhance it, including whether audit firms should be subject to term limits. It aimed at the tenure term of more than ten years and on the sustainability of rotation for the largest issuers.

It is a fact that tenure term limits present considerable operational charges. Opponents of mandatory term limits give practical difficulties few companies could face in finding a new independent auditor competent in the relevant industry, educating them in the company's business and financial reporting systems.

iii.   Audit Transparency

The third initiative taken by PCAOB relates to audit transparency. The Board amendments to its auditing to improve audit transparency by enhancing disclosure about the participants in audits, including disclosure about the partner in charge of the audit, as well as other firms involved in the audit. The Board needs to decide whether the Board should require engagement partners to sign audit reports.

The proposal would provide investors disclosure about other accounting firms and certain other participants in the audit. Increased transparency into the composition of cross-border audits should help investors gain a better understanding of how an audit was conducted and make more informed decisions about how to use the audit report.

12.2.2 Joint inspections, investor protection and the future

Audits are global both because companies are multi-national. Companies, whether multi-national or not, are increasingly seeking capital by listing outside their home-market.

Foreign companies listing in the United States have dramatically increased. Twenty percent of the companies listed on the New York Stock Exchange hail from abroad. Fifty of the 100 largest companies on the NYSE ae foreign. Moreover, listings by foreign companies on exchanges outside their home country are up everywhere.

The commitment to abide by the standards and laws of a strict investor protection regime rewards companies located in markets without developed investor protection regime. This helps a better cost of capital even in their home markets.

It is likely that audit reports for multi-national companies are signed by one audit firm, that firm will refer relevant work to its local affiliates in countries where the audit client has operations. These affiliates may be separate legal entities. In case they audit or play a substantial role in an audit, they will be separately registered with the PCAOB.

To summarise, the global network are neither too big nor small, but they are too important to leave unregistered. The PCAOB's relationship with CPAB to be a model of investor protection will work through intersecting and overlapping regulatory oversight of global audits.

Chapter 13

The Future of Audit: Technology

Introduction

Technology is bringing about many changes in how we live, work and interact. It becomes important for the audit profession to keep pace with the change and to understand how new technology trends can transform the audit approach.

Klaus Schwab, the Founder and Executive Chairman of the World Economic Forum, in January 2016 said that we are entering a fourth industrial revolution characterised by a range of new technologies that will alter the way we live, work and relate to one another. There have been technological advances in areas such as artificial intelligence, robotics, the Internet of Things, autonomous vehicles, 3-D printing, nanotechnology, biotechnology and quantum computing to name a few, those could transform every industry in every country.

There is wide debate around the impact the advances in technology will have on the scope of audit of the future. The profession of auditing will become less relevant if we don't engage with these developments. Though the pace of change will be perceived as a significant threat by many, however this is a time of great opportunity for the profession to embrace it.

Some roles will undoubtedly be eliminated, still there will always be need for skilled, human auditors who can apply sound judgment. The questions

such as, who will decide what information should be fed into technology enabled tools? Who will interpret and communicate the results? Who will ensure that end users can rely on the output from these tools and have a robust understanding as to how risks such as cyber threats have been mitigated?

13.1 Role of stakeholders in the future of Audit Technology

All stakeholders such as audit firms, regulators, companies and investors must engage and collectively drive forward the transformation to move towards the future technology.

a. Auditors

All audit firms need to build awareness and engage in the debate, as well as develop an agile strategy as key to successfully adapt to new technologies and opportunities. There is a responsibility on large audit firms to continue to invest in developing increasingly technologically enabled audits.

Increasing use of technology will result in new challenges for business and new risks in the audit process.

b. Audit Profession

Professional bodies should encourage and facilitate the dialogue needed to allow auditors to embrace the use of technology. There should be professional training and development requirements to adapt to the changing skills required of audit and accounting professionals.

c. Regulators and Standard Setters

Regulators need to work with audit firms to understand the experiments in progress and to make regulatory changes to regulatory requirements which will shape individual firm methodology.

If we want something meaningful to happen, we must ensure that we do not simply try and shoehorn the new technology into an existing framework. There needs to be a transparent process and mechanism for developing these new frameworks with inputs from all key stakeholders.

d. Companies

Boards and audit committees will need to be appropriately resourced and sufficiently trained to understand the impact of technology on financial reporting process.

e. Stakeholders

The investor community needs to be clear on the type of information needed, when it is needed and what the level of assurance required.

13.2 Current Technology Scenario

Technology is already changing the face of the audit profession and machines are helping us to do audits faster and with less risks.

a. Analytics

Improvements in analytics capabilities have allowed auditors with 24/7 analysis of a huge data sets. Also, testing complete data sets rather than a sample-based approach and a continuous audit is attainable with analytics. This will allow auditors to test audit evidence in real time, with timely identification of issues and allowing focus on anomalies in a population.

Further, audit analytics has an essential role in raising the audit quality bar, thus enabling stratification of data and focused testing of large or complex set of data sets. There is further shift towards predictive analytics – thus using analytics capabilities to predict events, explain when and why they might occur using modelling and simulation and thus give the most effective path to maximise opportunities.

b. Artificial Intelligence

AI is the task of getting computers and machines to do jobs those require human intelligence. Most AI is narrow and created to deliver a specific task within certain programmed parameters. This shows AI is reliant on human resources providing initial instructions and algorithms.

Cognitive computing uses artificial intelligence and machine learning algorithms to go beyond analytic capabilities and to learn and make autonomous decisions. The audit profession is also exploring the opportunities for harnessing AI within an audit approach. These new emerging technologies like AI present audit profession with many opportunities to improve the way we work to provide better services in a more efficient way.

To illustrate, auditors are now able to quickly process, highlight and extract key information from electronic documents. These cognitive capabilities help the auditor to assess a far broader population in totality and focus on major items of interest while the repetitive judgement area is automated.

The real changes of the audit profession will occur as these exponential coverages are combined with new technological disruptions often referred to as blockchain.

c. Blockchain

Blockchain or distributed ledger is the concept of a secured, distributed ledger of information which gives a platform for representing and exchanging things of value that could disrupt the way in which the transactions are conducted and recorded in the future.

The blockchain provides an immutable record of a transaction established in code. Few have suggested the future possibility of triple entry accounting where every accounting transaction recorded by an entity has a corresponding posting into a blockchain. The system becomes more transparent by design as all the transactions on a public distributed ledger are available to all the users in the network.

When seen in reality, this is not that practical and is dependent on collaboration within a complex ecosystem of companies, regulators, standard setters and government. The practical approach is that some core building blocks of the blockchain concept will be incorporated into the way in which private group of companies' function.

To illustrate, blockchain can be used to record small contracts between entities. It is easy to see the advantages of users being able to interact with smart contracts to invite automatic execution of defined rules and as a way of securely holding and transferring legal title of the asset. This would bring congruence between the recognition of costs in one entity and recognition of revenue in the other. Such transactions are self-relying meaning that the person auditing the recognition of revenue from the contract would know that the other party to the contract has agreed the costs incurred, either by themselves or through a trusted source of verification.

In the long term view, if we put the smart contracts and the triple entry accounting together, the world of auditing will look different. By placing all transactions verified by an independent source and a complete history of all transactions on the blockchain, the focus of an auditor can move from the audit of transactions in a year to auditing the terms of the smart contract itself.

Instead of waiting until year-end to see the impact of an entity's transactions on their financial statements, auditing could occur as small contracts are created before the transactions even take place. Misstatements due to fraud or error are stopped before they occur. This makes auditing real and not an annual event and thus bringing a new lens to transparency and corporate reporting.

The developmental efforts using distributed ledgers remain highly experimental and large scale commercial solutions have yet to emerge. We can say blockchain is still a relatively early stage technology.

13.3 Impact on the Audit

New technological tools have the potential to analyse large volumes of structured and unstructured data related to a company's information.

The major accounting firms believe that the use of these tools will enhance the audit by automating time-consuming tasks which are more manual in nature. To illustrate, through the use of artificial intelligence, robotic systems to interface with a client's systems to transfer and compile data automatically. Other areas where such technologies may be used include processing of confirmation responses or using drones for physical inventory observations.

This will give more time to the auditor to carefully examine the more complex and higher risk areas that require increased auditor judgement. Data analytics will allow auditors to better track and analyse their client's trends against industry or geographical databases. This will allow them to make better decisions.

However, the use of these technological tools raise certain challenges. It is important that the data being used is reliable, complete and accurate. Data security and quality control are also factors for firms to consider. Lastly, auditors need to be careful that they are not relying on data analytics. However powerful, these tools may be expected to become, they are not the substitutes for the auditor's knowledge and judgement.

For these technological tools and methods to help uphold the relevancy and timeliness of the audit, a higher quality audit needs to be developed and used to better serve the interests of the investors.

13.4 Impact on the future of the audit

It is yet to be determined how these technological advancements will shape the future of the audit.

Few are of the opinion that the audit of the future will be able to provide a greater level of assurance than today's level of 'reasonable assurance' as auditors may be able to examine 100 percent of a client's transactions. Others predict that the auditor's ability to access client's data in a timelier, standardised format may result in auditors moving towards a more continuous auditing approach.

The auditors will be able to amass a wide range of information and can go beyond the financial statements such as cybersecurity and sustainability reporting. Further, the increased automation and the use of artificial intelligence in audits may mean that firms will look to hire fewer junior auditors who previously performed the task manually which are now automated.

It is also heard that the challenges facing the future of the audit will come from the Googles of the world and the technological innovators in Silicon Valley which may make the offerings of the firms of today less relevant or can make the creative adaptive firms more relevant.

Therefore, it is extremely important for the current accounting students i.e. the future auditors to be knowledgeable about this evolving world of technology. Firms are on the lookout for top talents who possess abilities in science, technology, engineering and mathematics along with the ability to work with large quantities of data and possess analytical skills.

Chapter 14

A day in auditor's journey

Eyeing what an auditor has to do

Introduction

We have learnt that auditing is the process of investigating information prepared by someone else in order to determine whether the information is fairly stated. In case you are a business owner, you are responsible for the audited information which is presented in the financial records. In case you are the auditor, you investigate the assertions made on the financial statements to make sure what the company is saying is true and fair.

14.1 Secret lives of an auditor

As an auditor, you investigate the assertions that a company makes on its financial records. Although an auditor's life is nothing glamorous, however it can somewhat be exciting looking through a company's records and uncovering relevant information. Financial statements assertions often relate to how the company conducts business, how it handle its finances and spends money, how it manages its products and how it manages its employees. It further includes how it records financial information about its assets and liabilities, its equity and cash and investments.

Initially, a person aspiring to be an auditor may assume that auditing is a boring, repetitive job. A novice article may have to do a lot of grunt work like looking at invoices and reconciling documents. However, along the way, as an auditor digs through the records of the company, lot of fascinating information is discovered as to how different businesses operate. Every business that is audited provides new knowledge that helps one to get better at the job.

a. Exploring the ever changing business environment

The circumstances under which businesses operate have changed drastically over the last couple of decades. The advent of e-commerce and technological advances brought in business-to-business (B2B) and Business- to- consumer (B2C) commerce has allowed businesses to connect electronically with one another and with their customers. This has brought change in the functioning of businesses. The businesses have started outsourcing tasks such as human resources and inventory management, allowing companies to conduct business in any part of the world via internet and thus eliminating the need of shipping paper documents.

The question is how does it affect the auditors. In the past, the auditors relied on paper trains to examine the authenticity of the financial documents, these trails are increasingly electronic now. Electronic data can be manipulated specially where controls are lacking and more difficult to track down than a piece of paper and thus increased use of technology can render investors confused about the working and profitability of the business. It is the auditor's opinion that the outside entities more rely on regarding the authenticity of the financial information.

As more and more businesses are relying on the technological means to store, retrieve and transmit company data and documents, the auditor must stay aware of the advances in the latest accounting and business softwares, electronic connectivity and the way companies handle their accounts. The use of paper documents may be soon a thing of the past In order to stay competitive and provide quality audit, the knowledge of the latest computer systems and auditing programs is needed.

An auditor must be able to audit through the computer, which means evaluating internal controls and tracking accounting records in an electronic data processing system.

b.Working along the world economy

It is seen more small businesses are doing businesses globally due to technological advances. Hence, auditors with a knowledge of international accounting and standards on ethics and auditing used by other countries are in huge demand. With the economy being weak, there are chances that unethical clients can show higher profits than they actually earned to satisfy shareholders. An auditor has to keep a stalk of the situation.

14.2 Knowing major auditing concepts

The following four auditing concepts given below as required in every financial audit you conduct will give you a better taste of what auditing is about.

a. Materiality meaning not everything is important

Materiality is the importance you place on financial statements based on its overall significance. In case your client has omitted certain facts from its financial statements, it depends how much significant is the omission in comparison to the whole.

What is important is what is material to one client may not be material to another depending upon the size of the organization. It will help you to judge whether the omission or material misstatements is truly significant or no

b. Audit Evidence

Audit evidence are facts considered during the audit and that you record in the auditing working papers. It is the duty of the auditor to collect enough sufficient evidence while performing audit procedures that gives a reasonable basis for forming an opinion regarding financial statements under review.

c. Audit Risks

Every audit contains risk of providing an inappropriate opinion on the financial statements you are auditing. The major risk is that when the financial statements contain a material misstatement that you don't discover, or when the financial statements are correct but you state that they don't meet the standards.

d. Audit Sampling meaning looking at a bit of everything

It is not possible to look at all client's records. Your job as an auditor is to pick up a sample of client's records that you feel fairly represents the entire population of records. This sample is used as an evidence to back up your opinion on the financial statements.

14.3 Establishing Code of conduct

The following code of conduct is expected for you to follow as an auditor:

a. Integrity

Integrity as per auditing means you act according to code or standard of values. It means you serve your clients to the best of your abilities, keeping in mind that doing so may not be the same thing as completely agreeing with your client's financial statements. You need not worry that the client will express his displeasure with you if you disagree with the information in its financial statements.

Auditors must follow specific rules, standards or guidance. In order to show integrity, you must follow both the form and spirit of technical and ethical standards. Form means tangible and you need to follow the letter of the law. Spirit refers to implied facts.

As an auditor, in case you only follow the form of the technical and ethical standards that apply to your job without following the spirit of those standards, then you are not acting with integrity. For example, in case you have had adequate training to handle a specialised aspect of your client's audit but you don't really understand what you were taught in training, you are following the form but not the spirit of being able to professionally conduct the audit.

b. independence and objectivity

Being independent while providing auditing services means that you have no special relationship with or financial interest in the client that would cause you to disregard evidence and facts when evaluating your client. An auditor is required to be independent in both fact and appearance. For instance, you can't own a company that your child owns. In case you do, the people reading it will doubt its fairness.

An auditor needs to be objective meaning impartial, intellectually honest and free of conflict of interest.

- **Being impartial** means you are unbiased in all decision making process. You base your opinions on facts and not on any perceived notions.
- **Being intellectually honest** means you interpret rules and policies in truthful and sincere manner, staying both in form and spirit.
- **Free of conflict** means you don't perform services for any client whom you have either a personal or non-audited business relationship

c. Due Care

Due care means you plan and supervise adequately any professional activity for which you are responsible. For instance, as a staff auditor , you need to follow instructions of your team head and ask questions if something comes up during the course of the audit.

Competence means you have the education and experience to do the job and also a commitment to learning and professional improvement by taking continuing education classes throughout the career.

Diligence means you work to the best of your ability, showing concern for the best interest of the client while remaining consistent with your responsibility.

14.4 Getting Engaged: preparing to conduct an audit

An auditor should remember that just because a client comes to you and wants you to audit its financials, you are not obliged to accept the engagement. You are not selling clothes in a department, rather expressing an opinion on the fairness of the financial statements under audit. Lot of decisions are dependent on your audit report – decisions whether to invest in business or to extend your client credit.

It is your duty to make sure that you can provide a client with a quality audit before you can get started. The key is to fully understand your duties and responsibilities during the audit. The first duty is to make sure that the client's financial statements and reporting systems give you the information you need to ascertain that the financial statements are free from material misstatements. You also need to evaluate the possibility of your firm's reputation being tarnished through association with the potential new client.

However, the decision to accept new or continuing audit arrangements rests with the senior people. You as staff auditor need to only collect information for decision makers to review.

Following are the steps to be taken to collect information about a client so your firm can make an educated decision.

14.4.1. Learning about your client

In order to decide whether to accept new client or no, your audit firm has to answer two key questions:

Are you interested in working with the business?

Do you have the resources to perform the audit engagement?

It is important to know whether you have worked with this client before or no.

Every audit firm has a quality control system in place that gives procedures to be followed while learning about the client. Whether you have competent staff depends upon the unique facts of each potential client. If no one in your firm has experience of working in the client's industry or if the industry is unusual, your firm may not be adept enough to take on that audit.

You need to also assess the risk associated with accepting the audit engagement. For instance, the client should have a strong commitment to following generally accepted accounting principles and have adequate access to the books at your disposal so that you can do your job. If it is not, then you run the risk of either leaving the work half done or risk of not issuing a correct audit opinion.

You should also be sure that the client understands that the audit responsibilities aren't all on your part and you should document your discussions and the client's agreement in writing.

I. Assessing old clients

The process of determining whether to conduct a repeat audit begins when the previous audit is still underway. You can pretty easily tell during an audit if things are not going well. The auditor may question management's integrity or the competency of the financial records if a client's business seems to be shakier than it was in the previous year. This may make the auditor's firm, reluctant to accept another engagement.

In most cases, your clients stay steady from year to year and your firm continues to work with them. However, you need to reassess each client to look for any reason of concern. In case, such concerns are raised, you need to follow your firm's protocol for gathering information about the client's current status.. The information of how to assess a new client as given down will also apply here.

II. Assessing new client

While researching new client, you must gather as much information possible.

a. Meet with the client

The topics to be discussed with the client varies on how well you know the client. You need to discuss what services the client requires and whether your firm can fulfil them. You also need to find out whether the potential auditors have been audited in the past and if so, who conducted the audit.

At the end, the client should understand that before you accept the audit, you have to talk to the previous auditor and perform other pre-acceptance steps.

b. **Review existing records**

>   Its good to look at the previous year financial statements. This will give you a fair idea whether the financial records can be audited and whether the management is concerned with the sound accounting principles.
>
>   It is to be noted that the financial statements are the responsibility of the management. The auditor checks and gives his opinion on them thereon.

c. **Assess whether the client can be audited**

The condition of the financial statements offers clue to their auditability. By looking at the financial statements merely and realising they are in a mess, the auditor can make a decision whether to take up the client's work or no.

d. **Interviewing the previous auditor**

In case your potential client severe relations with the earlier auditor, you must get the client's permission to talk to the earlier auditor to know the exact reason of leaving and whether they encountered any problems regarding client's integrity, disagreements about how audit should be conducted, application of generally accepted accounting principles or lax internal controls.

In case your client doesn't give you permission, your firm may not want to accept the engagement. The client could be trying to cover up the fact that it is looking for a new auditor because the old auditor severed ties.

e. **Observing independence and objectivity with your client**

Independence and objectivity are closely related features that you need as an auditor. Independence means there is no relationship with the client that may affect your audit work. Objectivity means that the facts presented by the client is looked without prejudices.

While deciding whether to accept an auditing engagement, you must judge your independence and objectivity. In case your firm lacks independence or objectivity, you can't accept engagement.

Independence has to be in both fact and appearance. A conflict of interest, which affects independence at least in appearance, means that you have a personal or financial interest in the client, should not be accepted.

Following are few of the actual or perceived lack of independence:

- Your firm has an immediate family member working for or with the potential client.
- You or your firm has served in a management capacity with the potential client within the past few years or has provided appraisal, actuarial or valuation services to the client
- There is a direct or material indirect financial interest in the potential client. Direct interests are your partner

owning stock in the company or your firm having a loan to or from the potential client.

- Major portion of your firm's overall revenue comes from the same client. This creates a perceived lack of independence as your firm has a good reason to issue a favourable report.

The key is that the auditor must be unbiased and avoid any engagements that may lead users of the financial statements to question the auditor's independence. However, assessing firm independence isn't a decision you have to make until you reach the level of senior manager or partner at an auditing firm.

f. **Considering a client's integrity and competence**

Client's integrity needs to be judged before accepting an engagement. If the client lacks accounting kills and integrity, you should seriously consider not accepting the engagement.

Here are few of the areas which need to looked for evaluating a company's integrity:

- If the client has poor reputation in the community, then it is smarter to walk away from such clients.
- Inflated turnover may show unethical nature of business
- Checking whether any lawsuits are currently pending among the business owners. So, talking with lawsuit parties may show you vast amount of insider information that will affect your decision.
- If management has a bad attitude towards paying taxes, it's possible that revenue have been understated to lower the company's tax burden.

Moreover, if the company's management seems inept or the management is extremely inexperienced in the industry, it should be considered while making a decision to accept the engagement or not.

14.5 Understanding what services are required

It is important to know the requirements of the client and the procedures needed in preparing for an audit.

a. Finding out the requirements of the client

It is important to ask about the company's goals, its audit expectations and the specific purpose of the audit during the initial client interview. You can tell the client the nature of services offered by you. You may realise the company doesn't need the full blown financial statements audit. It is possible company may require only specific agreed upon procedures : engagements in which you issue reports only on specific subjects. For instance, you may be asked to confirm the cash on deposit or the valuation of the ending physical inventory.

Your goal at this point is to find out as many specifics as possible so your firm can determine whether it can meet those needs. You need to also find out about the client's reporting deadlines to make sure you can finish the work on time.

b. Tailoring audit procedures to each job

Next step is to plan the nature, timing and extend of the audit program.

Nature means the type of procedures you use during the audit and the method you use to gather sufficient, competent evidence to support the company's information. First thing is vouching means matching detailed accounting records to source documents. Second thing is physical examination, which means verification of an asset, like machinery whether it truly exists.

Timing tells when to do the audit procedures; before, on or after the balance sheet date. If the company is a continuing client, you should have the option to do some of your procedures during an interim visit before the balance sheet. Also, you are required to perform some procedures after the balance sheet date to address subsequent events that must be disclosed in the financial statements.

Extent refers to how deeply you have to dig in to the records. For instance, if you are checking out expenses, you decide how many expense vouchers you need to vouch. The higher the risk of error leading to material misstatements, the more the extent of your audit procedures.

14.6 Preparing the Engagement letter and entering into the contract

The engagement letter solidifies the audit arrangement between the audit firm and the client. It serves as a contract, detailing the duties and obligations on either side of the table. The audit firm prepares the engagement letter.

The engagement letter should be addressed to the board of directors in case of a corporation or to the chief executive officer if the client is a small concern. In case of a sole proprietorship, it should be addressed to the owner and partners in case of a partnership.

The topics to be covered in an engagement letter are:

- The purpose of the engagement i.e. the auditor needs to express an opinion on the financial statements
- The financial statements and application of the accounting principles is the responsibility of the management
- Limitations of the engagement i.e. as all the transactions are not examined, there's risk that material errors or frauds exist.
- The fees of the auditor and the time of payment

The engagement letter is eventually signed by the auditor and the client.

14.7 Knowing what to expect from the audit as part of the team

Initially, you are most likely to play the role of staff when you join an auditing firm. In case you do well, your promotional track will take you higher up the ladder. However, before you progress, you have to prove yourself as a brilliant staff associate.

a. **Your role in the audit team**

Each auditor takes responsibility for her/his particular task. Interaction with many different personalities and personal work ethics will help you develop your workplace interaction skills.

Normally, audit firm managers set the work schedules and senior associates assign tasks to staff associates. Staff associate tasks do the grunt work like:

- Ask clients for the invoices and other source documents
- Make sure the source documents match the financial statement balance
- To check invoices have been paid or customers have been billed
- Prepare schedules and workpapers

After the schedules and workpapers have been prepared, your senior associate will review it. The higher up you climb the ladder, the less you will audit. You will be delegating work, reviewing and sending out your own review notes to your associates.

b.Preparing workpapers and other audit documents

The job of a junior auditor is to prepare workpapers and schedules. Workpapers summarize your audit actions, such as planning the audit and schedules shows what steps are taken to reach a conclusion.

The auditing firm specifies how you will prepare all your audit documents. Its purpose, source of information and conclusions must be clearly evident.

The following elements must be considered while preparing workpapers:

- **A descriptive heading** should include the client's name, the purpose of workpaper and the date under examination
- **Indexing** means every workpaper shows unique page number like a book
- **Tick marks** as abbreviations for standard auditing tasks
- **Cross referencing** your workpapers to related and supporting workpapers to avoid duplication of workpapers
- **Source of information** to be sure to include what documents you examined or who was interviewed to collect audit evidence
- **Conclusion** means writing a summary of the results of your analysis and your opinion of the validity of the client assertion.

It's worth stating that all your documentation should be complete, concise and accurate. It should be so self-explanatory that your other colleagues can follow your calculations and understand how you reached them. Neatness is equally essential

14.8 Top ten procedures to obtain audit evidence

While working on any type of audit, you must gather sufficient competent evidence, which means collecting and reviewing enough client information to form a solid opinion of about whatever you are auditing. The following is the list of top ten procedures you use during an audit to obtain evidence. It is to be kept in mind that you can't use all ten at the same time.

Instead, you select the most appropriate ones for the auditing task at hand.

a. Inspection of records

The basic method of getting evidence is to ask your audit client for documents that support the assertions on its financial statements. For instance, for checking the correct recording of rent expense, you ask for all leases, paid invoices and other documents supporting the transactions.

You can use two of the things after having the records:

- **Tracing** means you first select a source document and then follow it to the books. It is a great test of management's complete assertion to see whether transactions taking place are recorded in the books correctly.
- For instance, to trace rent expense, you need to be ascertain if any lease needs to be capitalised-handled like fixed assets rather than straight expenses like rent expense
- **Vouching** is opposite to tracing – you first start with a transaction recorded in the books and follow it to the source of document. It tests the management assertion of occurrence. The source documents show you if what is recoded in the books actually happened.
- For example, there are few transactions affecting the rent expense account. They should be tracked forward to the associated leases and cash disbursements to make sure the client didn't make mistakes while entering them into the books.

b. Inspection of fixed assets

In order to inspect the fixed assets, you need to check whether the fixed assets actually exist. You need to be also sure that the assets you observe during your tour of the client's facilities show up on the books. In case your client maintains physical custody of securities and bonds, you confirm their existence by examining the certificate to make sure they reconcile to what's shown on the financial statements.

c. Recalculation

Recalculation means to check the mathematical accuracy of your client's computation. You use recalculation for checking invoices, journals, depreciation and other places where mathematical accuracy need to be checked.

d. Reperformance

Reperformance means checking whether the client is following his own established accounting and internal control procedures by doing the same task yourself. In case management approval is required to update any existing or new personal records, you need to check management is sign off on the initial document and you need to ascertain if the amendment in the financial records matches what management approved.

e. Ledger scrutiny

Ledger scrutiny is overall looking through the ledger to get an overall impression of the account's level of activity. While scrutinizing the ledger, an auditor can decide whether a detailed analysis of a particular account for further investigation is required rather than sample and test.

f. Observation

Observation means observing the employees perform the tasks and to see whether adequate internal controls are followed. For instance, as an auditor you can do a surprise check of the counting of inventory and whether finished goods and goods in progress are properly accounted for.

g. Enquiry

A major part of any type of audit is securing oral or written testimony from management, other employees and nonemployees like legal advisors.

In case a purchasing employee tells you that upper management has to sign off on all purchases over Rs 10000, you now have a benchmark for testing the internal control whether it is followed or no.

g. Confirmation

When you ask for written confirmation from outside parties regarding the accounts in the financial statements, it is also a way of collecting audit evidence. A good example is requesting accounts receivable information from customers. In this case, form letters are sent to customers to verify that the facts and figures contained in the client's books reconcile with the customers' facts and figures.

h. Analytical Procedures

Analytical procedures are adopted to compare what's on the books to what you expect to see on the book. It involves proper evaluation of financial information by studying possible relationships between financial and non-financial data and investigating fluctuations from previous year.

i. **Sampling**

It is not possible to look at all the client's records as it could be too cumbersome, time-consuming and costly. Instead, a sample of client records need to be selected that you feel it fairly represents the entire population of records. It can be used as sample as evidence to back up your opinion of the financial statements as a whole.

14.9 Tips to stay Educated in Audit procedures

Staying up-to-date with accounting, auditing and business developments keeps your skills sharp and enables you to provide quality service to your clients.

These are the tips to stay educated in audit procedures:

1. It is essential to keep updated with the current events and also auditing manuals.
2. It is crucial to attend accounting, auditing and business-related seminars to get relevant explanations of current events affecting how you do your job .Instead of official presentations on the standards , opt for an in-person lecture by an expert in the field who can break the topic into easy to understand sections. It is also good to have contacts in your field.
3. Continuing your education is important to keep your skills up-to-date.
4. Attending association meetings is also an important way of networking.

5. It is essential to stay update with the latest technology so you can work your audit more effectively and efficiently. The audit staff should be tech savvy to improve efficiency of work.

6. It is important to keep current with business model trends in your client's industry as understanding your client's environment allows you to effectively and efficiently work your audit from planning to reporting.

7. In order to provide excellent client services, you need to keep up with all new accounting software, thus reducing audit time, saving your firm money and client aggravation. For instance, you should stay current with electronic data retrieval systems so you can skilfully and quickly access client data stored in this manner.

8. Audit streamlining is required which involves reviewing prior-year audit data in a continuing client's permanent folder. In order to streamline, you must stay current with auditing software so you can more quickly and efficiently evaluate evidence and prepare and organise audit documents and working papers.

9. All auditors must current with what can be done by people trained in computer forensics accounting data for any type of audit engagement.

www.ingramcontent.com/pod-product-compliance
Lightning Source LLC
Chambersburg PA
CBHW021400210526
45463CB00001B/169